ASIA

in the

Undergraduate
Curriculum

ASIANetwork

**A CONSORTIUM OF LIBERAL ARTS COLLEGES
TO PROMOTE ASIAN STUDIES**

ASIANetwork is a consortium of about 150 North American colleges working together to strengthen the understanding and presence of Asia in liberal arts colleges. We believe that the liberal arts curriculum must incorporate within it a significant component of Asian Studies. This will help prepare a new generation of undergraduates for a changing world in which Asian societies will play prominent roles.

ASIANetwork thus responds to the need for Asian countries and cultures to be represented on our campuses and for our students and faculty to experience these cultures first hand. In a time of fiscal constraints, the Network has been created by member colleges to facilitate conversations among their faculty and administrators in the development of new programs, the strengthening of current ones, and the exploration of new opportunities for collaboration among institutions. The unique teaching mission, scale, and resource limitations of the undergraduate liberal arts institution pose special opportunities and challenges in the development of Asian Studies, and ASIANetwork aims to meet these needs.

ASIA
in the
Undergraduate
Curriculum

A Case for Asian Studies in Liberal Arts Education

Suzanne Wilson Barnett
and Van Jay Symons
Editors

AN EAST GATE BOOK

M.E. Sharpe
Armonk, New York
London, England

An East Gate Book

Library of Congress Cataloging-in-Publication Data

Asia in the undergraduate curriculum : a case for Asian studies in liberal arts education /
edited by Suzanne Wilson Barnett and Van Jay Symons.
 p. cm.
"An East Gate Book"
Includes bibliographical references and index.
ISBN 0-7656-0545-7 (cloth : alk. paper)—ISBN 0-7656-0546-5 (pbk. : alk. paper)
 1. Asia—Study and teaching. I. Barnett, Suzanne Wilson, 1940 — II. Symons, Van Jay.

DS32.8.A85   2000
950'.071'173—dc21   00-020161
                              CIP

Printed in the United States of America

The paper used in this publication meets the minimum requirements of
American National Standard for Information Sciences
Permanence of Paper for Printed Library Materials,
ANSI Z 39.48-1984.

BM (c)   10   9   8   7   6   5   4   3   2   1
BM (p)   10   9   8   7   6   5   4   3   2   1

We dedicate this book to all who have helped make a place
for Asia in the liberal arts.

Contents

Contributors   ix

Prologue
    Suzanne Wilson Barnett and Van Jay Symons   xi

1. Asia and the Undergraduate Curriculum
    Thomas B. Coburn   3

2. Asian Studies at American Private Colleges, 1808–1990
    Samuel Hideo Yamashita   23

3. Asian Language Study in Liberal Arts Colleges
    Stanley L. Mickel   52

4. Study Abroad in Asia
    Stephen P. Nussbaum   76

5. Remapping Asian Studies
    Rita Smith Kipp   98

6. Where We Came From, Where We Are Going
    Ainslie T. Embree   125

Bibliography   151

Index   161

Contributors

Suzanne Wilson Barnett is a China historian and professor of history at the University of Puget Sound. She is a graduate of Muskingum College and received her Ph.D. from Harvard University. She served on the ASIANetwork board of directors from 1996 through 1999, as chair in 1998–1999.

Thomas B. Coburn is a specialist in the religions and cultures of South Asia and is academic vice president and Charles A. Dana Professor of Religious Studies at St. Lawrence University. He did his undergraduate work at Princeton and received his Ph.D. from Harvard University. He served on the ASIANetwork board of directors in 1996–1999.

Ainslie T. Embree is a historian of South Asia and professor emeritus of history, Columbia University. His undergraduate degree is from Dalhousie University, and he received his Ph.D. from Columbia University. A past president of the Association for Asian Studies, he serves on the ASIANetwork council of advisors.

Rita Smith Kipp is an anthropologist with a specialty in Indonesia, and is a professor of anthropology at Kenyon College. She is a graduate of the University of Oklahoma and received her Ph.D. from the University of Pittsburgh. She served on the ASIANetwork board of directors in 1993–1996.

Stanley L. Mickel is professor in Chinese language and literature at Wittenberg University. His undergraduate degree is from the University of California, Berkeley, and he received his Ph.D. from Indiana University. He serves on the ASIANetwork board of directors from 1997 through 2000, as chair in 1999–2000.

Stephen P. Nussbaum is an anthropologist with a specialty in Japan, and is a professor at Earlham College, where he has been administrator of the Japan Study program. Beginning in 1999–2000, he is visiting professor at the Center for International Education at Waseda University, Tokyo. He did his undergraduate work at the University of Notre Dame and received his Ph.D. from Cornell University. He served on the ASIANetwork board of directors in 1993–1996.

Van Jay Symons is a China historian and professor of history at Augustana College. He is a graduate of Brigham Young University and received his Ph.D. from Brown University. He served on the ASIANetwork board of directors from 1995 through 1998, as chair in 1997–1998, and currently is executive director of ASIANetwork.

Samuel Hideo Yamashita is a Japan historian and Henry E. Sheffield Professor of History at Pomona College. His undergraduate degree is from Macalester College, and he received his Ph.D. from the University of Michigan.

Prologue

Suzanne Wilson Barnett and Van Jay Symons

This book explores the dynamic teaching and learning evidenced in liberal arts education, and it suggests that the study of Asia at the undergraduate level enriches and deepens liberal arts education. The book chronicles the growing awareness of the value of integrating coordinated courses on Asian life and thought into college curricula as a basis for enabling students to understand, and contribute to, an increasingly mobile world of diverse societies and cultures. Moreover, the book argues that the rich intellectual and cultural traditions of Asia enhance liberal arts education. The chapters that follow make a case for Asian studies in the liberal arts, but in the process they also make a case for the liberal arts.

Central to this book is the web of colleges brought together in recent years by ASIANetwork, a national consortium of more than 125 liberal arts colleges and small universities to promote the study of Asia at the undergraduate level. Founded in 1992, this organization is the manifestation of the liveliness of Asian studies in undergraduate study. In turn, through annual conferences, a newsletter, and grant-funded initiatives ASIANetwork has created opportunities for faculty at member institutions to expand their intellectual horizons and to work together toward pedagogical excellence, intellectual community across the campus and among institutions, and cross-cultural understanding.

The Henry Luce Foundation has supported the educational mission of ASIANetwork through two major grants, the second encompassing as one project the creation of this book. This support has enabled growing awareness of the variety of curricular, cocurricular, and off-campus programs in Asian studies found in America's colleges. Building on what is happening in the colleges, the editors and authors shifted early on to a conceptualization of the book as an illumination of principles that are fundamental to the shared enterprise of teaching and learning with emphasis on complex ideas and reflective practice.

With one exception the contributors to this book teach at liberal arts colleges that are longstanding members of ASIANetwork. The one exception, Ainslie T. Embree, professor emeritus, Columbia University, brings to the project a distinguished career of teaching and superb scholarship that have enhanced ASIANetwork, on whose council of advisors he is a pioneer member. Others whose work produced this book are from the following institutions: Augustana College (Van Jay Symons), Earlham College (Stephen P. Nussbaum), Kenyon College (Rita Smith Kipp), Pomona College (Samuel Hideo Yamashita), St. Lawrence University (Thomas B. Coburn), the University of Puget Sound (Suzanne Wilson Barnett), and Wittenberg University (Stanley L. Mickel). Among us are four historians (Barnett, Embree, Symons, and Yamashita), two anthropologists (Kipp and Nussbaum), one specialist in religious studies (Coburn), and one specialist in language and literature (Mickel). The chapter authors include two specialists in South Asian studies, two specialists in Japanese studies, one specialist in Chinese studies, and one specialist in Southeast Asian studies.

The authors of the chapters that make up this book had no roadmap; rather, they have responded brilliantly to the challenge of creating a book for which no precedent exists. Thomas Coburn's depiction of possibilities available to engender great teaching and learning focused on Asia leads naturally to Samuel Yamashita's original analysis of the history of Asia in the programs of small colleges in the United States. Stanley Mickel's investigation of the rise and dynamics of the study of Asian languages in the colleges moves toward Stephen Nussbaum's thoughtful examination of study abroad in Asia as a fundamental experience in liberal arts education. Rita Kipp's creative look at the "remapping" of teaching and learning about Asian peoples and cultures proceeds toward Ainslie Embree's focus on the symbiotic relationship of liberal arts education and Asian studies, now tied together as intimately as ever. The book concludes decisively that liberal arts education is alive with prospects at century's and millenium's end and a new era's beginning.

A pivotal meeting of authors and editors occurred in June 1998 in Colorado Springs. Discussions at this meeting contributed coherence to the volume while allowing each chapter author latitude in the definition and exploration of topic. The editors remain grateful for the creative and responsible efforts of the authors at the meeting, which also enjoyed the participation of Marianna McJimsey, Colorado College, then executive director of ASIANetwork, and Terrill Lautz, a China historian and vice president of the Henry Luce Foundation.

The Luce Foundation has taken a giant step toward the affirmation of the achievements and promise of both the study of Asia and the liberal arts through the inauguration of the new Luce Fund for Asian Studies. Over a four-year period commencing in 1999 the foundation will issue grants on a competitive basis to launch about ten junior-level professorships per year to strengthen Asian studies programs in selective American liberal arts colleges. These perhaps forty new faculty positions in Asian studies will bring added energy and intellectual power to far more than the institutions receiving the grants. They stand to make a resounding statement about the validity of knowledge shared across disciplines in the humanities and social sciences, as well as about the validity of the kind of teaching and learning that involves teachers and students in intensive encounter with multiple points of view.

We commend the chapters that follow and invite readers to reflect upon the meaning of the liberal arts and the appeal of Asian studies in the liberal arts context. One metaphor for liberal arts education may be found in the oft-cited ruminations of the ancient Chinese philosopher Zhuangzi, who danced in what Arthur Waley termed "the realm of nothing whatever." Zhuangzi asserted that in order to walk we need much more ground than that which is immediately beneath the landed foot.[1] By analogy, we cope better with the flights and folly of human existence to the degree that we have access to varied ways of thinking and can call upon a vast array of ideas. Underlying the very existence of ASIANetwork is the conviction that the complex traditions and historical experiences of Asian peoples hold elegant promise as part of the liberal education so important to the wise stewardship of our shared world.

> Suzanne Wilson Barnett, *University of Puget Sound*
> Van Jay Symons, *Augustana College*
> (Executive Director, ASIANetwork)

Note

1. See Arthur Waley, *Three Ways of Thought in Ancient China*, 3.

ASIA
in the
Undergraduate
Curriculum

1

Asia and the Undergraduate Curriculum

Thomas B. Coburn

In a general way, the place of the university in the culture of Christendom is still substantially the same as it has been from the beginning. Ideally, and in the popular apprehension, it is, as it has always been, a corporation for the cultivation and care of the community's highest aspirations and ideals. But these ideals and aspirations have changed somewhat with the changing character of Western civilization; and so the university has also concomitantly so changed in character, aims and ideals as to leave it still the corporate organ of the community's dominant intellectual interest. At the same time, it is true, these changes in the purpose and spirit of the university have always been, and are always being, made only tardily, reluctantly, concessively, against the protests of those who are zealous for the commonplaces of the day before yesterday. Such is the character of institutional growth and change; and in its adaptation to the altered requirements of an altered scheme of culture the university has in this matter been subject to the conditions of institutional growth at large. An institution is, after all, a prevalent habit of thought, and as such is subject to the conditions and limitations that surround any change in the habitual frame of mind prevalent in the community.

—Thorstein Veblen[1]

When the words quoted above were penned by their author, the year was 1918. What Veblen had in mind, among other things, we may surmise, was the tumultuous debates that had convulsed American higher education in the latter part of the nineteenth century, revolving around the new free elective system that Charles William Eliot advocated so relentlessly during the forty years of his presidency of Harvard (1869–1909) and that has had such a profound effect on college curricula ever since. But it is also possible he saw beyond that lengthy episode to the antecedents of the controversy in the Enlightenment, for, as W.B. Carnochan has keenly noted, "'Ancients' and 'moderns' take their names originally from the 'battle of the books' fought in the late seventeenth and early eighteenth centuries between defenders of ancient literature and learning and defenders of, among things, the new science."[2]

Veblen's analysis can be extended prospectively as well, for it was in the following year that Columbia University's Contemporary Civilization course was first established, a collaborative venture between economics, government, philosophy, and history to serve as a common core, an antidote to the rampant elective spirit.[3] A similar yearning appeared in the roughly contemporaneous "Great Books" vision of Robert Maynard Hutchins, which "merged the history of Western civilization with that of its great books," to which the famous Harvard Redbook of 1945 (*General Education in a Free Society*) served as a kind of riposte.[4] Add to these episodes the "culture wars" of the past decade, fueled by the growing possibility, originating in anthropology, that "culture" is not a singular but a plural phenomenon, and Carnochan's claim seems persuasive: "There have always been ancients and moderns, and lines of allegiance may be generational as much as intellectual. If Western philosophy is a series of footnotes to Plato, the pedagogical debate of the past few years has been a series of footnotes to the several battles of the books that began with Bacon's proposals for the 'advancement of learning,' his program for the overturning of Scholasticism and for an empirical conquest of the natural world."[5]

In this context, where the study of Asia might now appear as a potential upstart, a relative newcomer in the centuries-long battle over the substance of university education, how might we best situate Asian studies in the curricula of private liberal arts colleges? Is this emergence of Asian studies simply another turn of the cyclical wheel of curricular debate, eventually to give way to an as yet unknown successor, or is something more substantial, more enduring at stake here?

It is my judgment, shared by my fellow contributors to this volume, that Asian studies is not a mere passing fancy, that something of surpassing significance is afoot here, and that all who care about contemporary education must pay attention. Moreover, what is at stake is of consequence not just for higher education, but for the "habitual frame of mind" of the larger community that is correlated with the life of the university every bit as much today as it was in Veblen's day. If we can get clear about why the study of Asia is so important, especially in the liberal arts colleges of America, then those institutions can continue to provide the leadership—and the leaders—for which our country and our world so ache today. Historically the liberal arts colleges of America have not simply been mirrors or microcosms of the larger ebb and flow of American social and cultural life, as Veblen's analysis might imply. They have stood in a dialectical relationship to the surrounding society, provoking and inspiring as well as reflecting it. Although liberal arts colleges are few in number and size, constituting less than 5 percent of American institutions of higher education with less than 2 percent of the student enrollment, they have had an influence out of all proportion to their numbers. This continues to be the case in important, often neglected ways. For instance, of the 30 institutions producing the highest ratio of doctoral to bachelor's degrees in their alumni, 16 are private liberal arts colleges.[6] Liberal arts colleges produce Rhodes and Marshall scholarship winners at a rate per number of bachelor's degrees awarded that is nearly double that of research universities. As of 1990, 9.4 percent of the nation's foreign service officers and 10.4 percent of its ambassadors were liberal arts college graduates.[7] If we can discern and articulate the importance of Asian studies in the liberal arts college curriculum, we shall have done something of potential usefulness not just for Asianists and for Asians, but for those more broadly engaged in contemporary education as well.

To make such a case is the burden of this chapter. The broad gauge introduction up to this point has been intentional, for unless we wish absolute inclusivity in our college curricula—a vision that even the most well-endowed university cannot realize today—then no subject matter that clamors for inclusion in the curriculum, including Asian studies, should be exempt from the requirement of self-consciously positioning itself in relationship to the larger educational goals of the institution. I shall therefore pursue these broad matters further in the following section, with some additional reflections on contemporary liberal arts education, many of which will be seen to have implications for Asian studies. Then I shall turn to consider the place of the study of Asia in the Western academy generally, without regard for the particular kind of educational institution. Finally, I shall bring these considerations to bear on strategies for increasing Asian studies in that uniquely American institution, the private liberal arts college.

Asia and Liberal Arts Education

For the past thirty years a recurrent metaphor has been employed to describe the multifaceted struggles to reform college curricula. It has been employed by both proponents and opponents of reform, both ancients and moderns. This is the metaphor of "decentering" the curriculum. What this means specifically varies from context to context, but it has been applied variously to such matters as the interest in popular history as opposed to that of elites; to women's issues as opposed to men's; and to African American, African, Asian, or Hispanic literature as opposed to "Western"—and the list could be extended. Wherever concern for issues of race, class, and gender has been raised, it has been seen as a destabilizing presence, alternatively seen as a cause for celebration or for alarm. "Things fall apart; the centre cannot hold," declared William Butler Yeats.[8] And so the academy has agreed, pursuing the implications of this discovery with either joy or terror ever since.

But has there ever actually *been* a center? Granted that each of the decentering initiatives has had a specific conception of its antagonist and of what needs displacement, and granted that each of those antagonists has had a specific conception of the educational center that warrants defense, one still needs to ask the question, has there been an enduring core to liberal education? Veblen and Carnochan, who have already oriented us to this inquiry, suggest on historical, not ideological, grounds that the answer to this question is no, there is no abiding essence or center to liberal education. There is an ongoing concern for intellectual training and critical thinking, often linked with specific subject matter and a concern with education for informed citizenship, but subject matters change, as does the meaning of citizenship. There is no linear continuity to the liberal arts tradition, no essence.[9] I suggest, therefore, that the metaphor of decentering—and its assumption that a center exists—be dropped from discussions of educational curricula and of the broader goals of liberal education.

In its stead I propose an alternative metaphor, also drawn from the realm of geometry. It is the *ellipse*, and I intend this metaphor to be understood in the very specific way that an ellipse differs from a circle. A *circle* is defined as the pattern that one point traces when it revolves around another point so that it is always equidistant from that point. That reference point, of course, is the circle's center. An *ellipse* is defined as the pattern that one point traces when it revolves around *two* other points so that the sum of its distances from those two points remains a constant. Those two reference points are known as the foci of the ellipse.

The virtue of this metaphor, I have found, apart from the fact it gets us away from the chimerical notion of there being a single center to the educational process, is that it invites us to think of the curriculum, and of education more broadly, in terms of balance, of point and counterpoint, of constructive tensions between antinomies that cannot be overcome, of dyads in a dialectical relationship, neither of whose members can be reduced to the other. Once this metaphorical door is open, then a host of possible applications come tumbling through. For instance, one might identify the two foci of liberal education as curricular and extracurricular, or as major requirements and distribution requirements/general education, or as major program and minor. One might suggest that the way *content* and *skills* consistently and mutually implicate one another reflects their role as the two foci of the curriculum. Teaching and research are obvious candidates for the two complementary emphases in faculty life. Conventional classroom learning can be seen as juxtaposed with an alternative focus, such as service learning or study abroad or internships. In a highly regarded little article, which also happily uses an Asian metaphor, Elizabeth Blake suggests that academic affairs and student affairs offices attract different personality types, offer different assessments of formal learning, envision opposite learning outcomes, and have differing perceptions of power. But rather than striving to be more alike, they should be seen as "The Yin and Yang of Student Learning in College."[10] It is this same "elliptical" way of thinking that has prompted me to suggest that an effective way of teaching survey courses on Asia is to juxtapose the "Great Tradition" of textbooks with units of "contemporary counterpoint" that introduce very different perspectives and content, throwing the alternative assumptions of both perspectives into bold relief and teaching through contrast.[11] One way to do justice to the energy and vibrancy that characterize our campuses, then, is to conceptualize the tensions as the necessary and creative manifestations of an ellipse's two foci, variously manifested, rather than as the compulsive search for a single, monolithic center, which is never to be found, either historically or ideally.

There are additional reasons for preferring this binary understanding of the educational process. One is epistemological, the fact that we now know that the basis for much learning, if not all, is comparative. We distinguish between different objects "out there" on the basis of similarity, contrast, and analogy. It is in the juxtaposition and analysis of apparently similar or apparently different data that we deepen our understanding of all of them, that we test the validity of those appearances. This holds true whether we are seeking to understand biological fauna or political systems or cultural creations. As Jonathan Z. Smith has pithily noted, "In Comparison, a Magic Dwells."[12] That magic is the magic at first of perceiving, then of knowing, and eventually of understanding.

A second corollary reason for thinking of liberal education as a binary, dialectical process follows immediately. One of the "objects" we are trying to understand, and to help our students understand, is ourselves, both individually and in terms of the groups, cultural and other, to which we belong. The traditional way of putting this is to say that liberal education aspires to raise students out of the parochialism of particularity, to free them from the singularity of their own experience. The postmodern phrasing of a similar point is that we aspire to help students become aware of their own positionality and subjectivity, to develop their own voice while learning to understand and appreciate others. In either case, the challenge is great because of the inevitable affection for one's own perspective and the subtle, transparent way in which the knower's perspective is unwittingly operative in all acts of knowing. It is uncommonly difficult to become alert to differential power relationships when one's own position of privilege is at stake. There exists no better way for "problematizing" one's own or one's students' subjectivity than through deliberate engagement with people and cultures that offer powerful contrasts to the would-be knowers' starting-point.[13] William Perry's now famous scheme suggests that students start their college careers with a "basic duality" in their engagement with the world, and that the challenge of the college years is to help them move from this dualism through relativism to commitment.[14] Vital engagement with cultural difference can play a crucial role in effecting students' intellectual and moral development. As Claude Levi-Strauss reminds us, for both "insiders" and "outsiders," cultural artifacts are wonderful "goods to think with."[15]

The utility of dualistic thinking for understanding both oneself and cultural differences is not just an epistemological claim nor, heaven forbid, a political assertion. It is empirically grounded, and much of the emerging literature on the educational benefits of engaging diversity has very direct implications for Asian studies. The American Association of Colleges and Universities (AAC&U) has done groundbreaking work of late in advancing contemporary discussion of diversity beyond the politics of race, ethnicity, and affirmative action to ask more fundamental questions about the *educational* consequences of diversity. Below are some of the conclusions emerging from the AAC&U's recent review of the research literature, *Diversity Works: The Emerging Picture of How Students Benefit*. Although emphasizing racial diversity, these conclusions have clear ramifications for other measures of diversity, including the cultures and peoples of Asia.

> Overall, the literature suggests that diversity initiatives positively affect both minority and majority students on campus. Significantly, diversity initiatives have an impact not only on student attitudes and feelings toward intergroup relations on campus, but also on institutional satisfaction, involvement, and academic growth. . . .
>
> The evidence continues to grow that serious engagement of issues of diversity in the curriculum and in the classroom has a positive impact on attitudes toward racial issues, on opportunities to interact in deeper ways with those who are different, on cognitive development, and on overall satisfaction and involvement with the institution. These benefits are particularly powerful for white students who have had less opportunity for such engagement. . . .
>
> Evidence in the literature suggests that comprehensive institutional change in teaching methods, curriculum, campus climate, and institutional definition provides educational benefits for minority and majority students. Comprehensive diversity initiatives, beyond their capacity to improve access and retention for underrepresented groups, are related to satisfaction, academic success, and cognitive development for *all* students.[16]

To the extent, then, that the primary challenge of the human future is learning to live with those who are both similar to and different from ourselves, the study of Asia—which is *itself* dauntingly diverse—can contribute in rich and unparalleled ways.

One final general point on liberal arts education. Alongside the curricular debates of recent years, revolving around the question of the appropriate content of college curricula, there is another debate centering on the appropriate pedagogy for delivering any curriculum. Given the exponential growth in knowledge, so the argument goes, and the dismal long-term retention that students show of *any* subject matter, ought we not to limit our aspirations to comprehensive coverage, emphasize the constructed nature of all knowledge, and use vivid examples to help students understand specifically how the construction process works in different settings? Ought not the brilliant lecturer, the "sage on the stage," give way to the Socratically mentoring "guide by the side"? Such a question is by no means merely rhetorical, particularly in the natural sciences, where the felicitously phrased "lust for coverage" that Ainslie Embree and Carol Gluck see as the "deadliest sin" in the teaching of world history, is comparably rampant.[17] Yet even in the sciences there is important contrary evidence, perhaps most vividly apparent in the work of Project Kaleidescope, that demonstrates that it is hands-on, research-rich, lab-based science instruction from which students learn most and that they find most gratifying.[18] It is a similar impulse that has recently produced inquiry-based and problem-based learning in a great variety of disciplines. The moral for our purposes, therefore, is that the sheer massiveness of the subject matter that Asia provides ought not to be an obstacle to its incorporation into the curriculum. One need not study the whole of Asia in order to study it responsibly. It is precisely this intuition that is beginning to produce such enormously useful material as *Case Studies in the Social Sciences: A Guide for Teaching*, a volume in the Columbia Project on Asia in the Core Curriculum, which invites faculty in anthropology, economics, political science, and sociology to make use of Asian examples without, in the process, having to becoming Asianists.[19] We will return to this matter of specialists and nonspecialists below.

Asian Studies and the Academy

There are two primary reasons for including the study of Asia in the Western academy today. The first has to do with the unparalleled richness of the subject matter. The second has to do with the transitional moment in world history at which we currently find ourselves.

The first point is simple and can be made on a combination of cognitive and moral grounds, where the moral leverage is exerted on our obligations both to today's students and to Asians, past and present.

If one thinks only in the grossest terms of the world's major civilizations, one notices that four of them grew on Asian soil: Indian, Chinese, Japanese, and Islamic. If one considers the old adage about Western civilization being produced by the marriage between Athens and Jerusalem, then at least half of what we call "the West" is, in fact, Asian. Moreover, in looking at the ostensibly non-Asian partner in that mar-

riage, one finds that "the Greeks and the Romans had their major connections not northward (until quite late in the Roman Empire) but east-
ward where, they realized, most of the wealth and the sophisticated ideas
came from."[20] There is therefore real historical appropriateness in the
title of a world map that hung on a classroom wall throughout my graduate
studies. It was "Asia and Surrounding Regions." If at least one of the
goals of liberal education is to expose students to the richness of the
human heritage—to the sphere of "humane literacy," in Stanley
O'Connor's lovely phrase—then any education that ignores Asia will
be woefully inadequate.[21] It is only a myopic obsession with "Western
culture" in a narrowly constructed and recent sense that could justify
the exclusion of Asia from the liberal arts curriculum.

Let me give a single example of the richness of evidence that Asia
presents. One of the greatest adventures in all of human history is the
story of how Buddhism found its way from India to East Asia. The fact
that the Chinese were able to "make sense" of Buddhism is astonishing,
an extraordinary instance of cross-cultural communication, in light of
the striking contrasts between the two classical traditions. Arthur Wright
puts the issues this way:

> In their attitudes toward the individual the two traditions were poles apart.
> . . . The Chinese had shown little disposition to analyze the personality
> into its components, while India had a highly developed science of psy-
> chological analysis. In concepts of space and time there were also strik-
> ing differences. The Chinese tended to think of both as finite and to reckon
> time in life-spans, generations, or political eras; the Indians, on the other
> hand, conceived of time and space as infinite and tended to think of cos-
> mic eons rather than units of terrestrial life.
>
> The two traditions diverged most critically in their social and political
> values. Familism and particularistic ethics continued to be influential
> among the Chinese even in an age of cataclysmic change, while Mahayana
> Buddhism taught a universal ethic and a doctrine of salvation outside the
> family. Whereas Chinese thinkers had long concentrated their efforts on
> formulas for the good society, Indian . . . thought had laid particular stress
> upon the pursuit of other-worldly goals.[22]

What extraordinary grist for the intellectual mill is found in this passage! There is not a discipline in the humanities or social sciences that
could not sink its analytic teeth into the substance of the issues here—
and although Wright does not say so, this Asian episode also raises fundamental, liberal arts kinds of issues in the arts as well. Note also that it

is Asian subject matter *itself* that raises these issues, without even beginning to raise the question of comparison with Western assessment of the same issues.

But, one might argue, all this is past history. While part of contemporary liberal education must attend to the question of our human heritage and should therefore include Asian content, that can only be a part of today's curriculum—and, moreover, today's students are notoriously averse to topics that lie outside their contemporary ken. An answer to this objection is growing more obvious by the day. It starts from the observation that nearly 60 percent of the world's population today resides in Asia. It proceeds to a differential analysis of how wealth is distributed globally, where the internal evidence from Asia varies enormously and, as the events of the recent past remind us, huge and as yet not fully understood forces are abroad, affecting all the economies of the world. Then the case for studying Asia as part of the contemporary world can be clinched around a salient feature of that world, namely, the way in which cultures and populations have become mobile in unprecedented ways, unhinging Asia and Asians from the geography of Asia and weaving them into other cultures and peoples and places around the globe, including North America. This, of course, is part of what the current American turmoil over "multiculturalism" is all about.

In her chapter for this volume, Rita Kipp will take up this issue of diasporas, culture flows, geography, and area studies more systematically. For our purposes, we should note two further developments that support the argument for Asian studies on the grounds of its contemporary relevance. First, the Ford Foundation, well known as the fiscal midwife of academic "area studies" during the 1950s, recently has directed a new initiative to colleges and universities under the title *Crossing Borders: Revitalizing Area Studies*. It expressly recognizes the need to find "new ways of conceptualizing 'area' [including Asia] so that its study opens up exciting new questions, new approaches, new ways of understanding both history and changes in the contemporary world." The goal is "to create a more truly international area studies in which scholars and practitioners (artists, activists, public intellectuals) from diverse 'areas' shape the agenda and formulate, from their perspectives, important questions about the relationships between regional and global experience."[23] In other words, the very benefactor that "more than any other private donor or government agency . . . played a significant role in launching and nurturing the field [of area studies] in the United States" is now challenging its practitioners to reconceive the field in light of changes in the dynamics and conception of global interaction.[24] The very way we think about "Asia," "Africa," "the Middle East" is today in flux, and a fresh vision of our work will be the joint construction of those who live within a given area and those who live "abroad." Second, perhaps the most persuasive case for thinking of Asian studies as part of the *American* scene has been made by Diana Eck. With assistance from the Lilly Foundation and a team of researchers, she has produced *On Common Ground: World Religions in America*, a CD-ROM designed as a teaching tool and based on a still-growing data base to help students—and their teachers—understand the new religious and cultural geography of America.[25] As a measure of the importance of this work, Eck was one of nine Americans selected by President Bill Clinton to receive the 1998 National Humanities Medal, which was presented in a ceremony at the White House on November 5, 1998. No liberal arts college in the country should be without *On Common Ground*, a powerful tool for understanding the new ways in which Asian studies has come to overlap with American studies.

The second imperative for including the study of Asia in the Western academy requires that we take a long view of the academy's history. This is just what the great historian of religion, Wilfred Cantwell Smith, did in his plenary address to the New York State Conference for Asian Studies held at Colgate University in 1975, under the title "The Role of Asian Studies in the American University."[26] Challenging the assembled Asianists by declaring that "the future of humankind does in fact depend on you more than it depends on most other sectors of our universities," Smith went on to develop the following thesis: "The Western university is in distress . . . and . . . we as students of Asia have a contribution to make to the self-understanding of the university as such; to the idea of rationality; and to the process and meaning of the human mind's endeavor to apprehend the universe and the human place in it and relation to it."[27] Smith reminds us of the two stages in the development of the Western university. In the first, "beginning in Europe in the early Middle Ages, . . . it [the university] was oriented to Western culture, its central task the preservation, nurture, transmission, and extrapolation of that culture." In the second, "developing out of the addition of science, [the university was] oriented to the natural world." The latter orientation actually grew out of the former but eventually became autonomous and established a new relationship to technology, "with knowledge aimed at prediction and control, and a pursuit of action." These two stages of the university's history, Smith argues, represent two different emphases or interpretations of rationality, two different understandings of what it means to be human that were "never quite integrated." During the first phase, the study of Asia occasionally appeared casually, as a by-product of curiosity about culture. During the second, it appeared more systematically, as part of the empirical, largely social scientific and strategic interest in area studies. What has now become apparent, Smith claims, is that "the study of Asian civilization is in fact too big an enterprise to fit within either of the extant orientations, or indeed in both of them together. It is showing itself, at least potentially, to be a *tertium quid*; or better, to transcend either, and indeed both. . . . The addition of Asian studies to the curriculum may turn out in the end to be as transforming as was the addition of the sciences."[28] I argued above that the massiveness of the subject matter that is Asia ought not to be an obstacle to inclusion in the college curriculum, because of the utility of case studies. It now turns out that it is precisely the massiveness of Asian subject matter that argues *for* its inclusion in the curriculum, because of its potential to move the Western academy beyond its inherited ways of understanding the world.

What Asian studies can redeem the contemporary academy from is its obsession with objectivity, its assumption that subjectivity is the only alternative. Smith challenges scholars thus: "The Western university does its work badly if it interprets Asia in purely objective, behaviourist, impersonalist terms, on the one hand, under the pretention of being 'scientific,' or if, on the other hand, it simply presents it in its own Asian terms, uninterpreted, receiving at face value and uncritically the self-understanding of an alien culture." Asian studies, sensitively done, is reflexive, always questioning the inherited concepts employed in the interpretation of Asian subject matter, refashioning one's conceptual tools to come to a more apt understanding. The study of Asia, furthermore, can redeem the contemporary academy from its preoccupation with discipline-based methodology, for it is inherently and necessarily interdisciplinary: "The notion 'interdisciplinary' offers a ladder for climbing out of a hole into which true scholars have never fallen."[29]

If anything, the seductiveness of theory and methodology in the academy has escalated dramatically in the quarter-century since Smith offered his challenge and so the tone of urgency, even alarm, in Anthony Reid's recent address to the Asian Studies Association of Australia is particularly striking. In speaking of the "alarming dominance of theory, in practice North American–driven and antithetical to regional expertise," he writes:

> Dethroning the canon of European classics written by dead white males has led not to a courageously pluralist exploration of the world's cultural and social diversity, but to a new (if swiftly changing) canon of self-referential theory. . . . The tendency of the older disciplines to become more theoretical, self-referential and impenetrable to outsiders is dangerous, not only to themselves but to students who must negotiate a fast changing, plural world. Area studies operations are increasingly precious as reservoirs of cross-disciplinary new ideas fashioned out of direct contact with difference.[30]

What is at stake, then, in making a place today for Asian studies in American colleges and universities is not just redressing the balance between "West" and "East," a conceptualization of vanishing validity. The core issue is not simply how best to prepare our students to live with the broadest horizons to their imaginations and understandings of citizenship, with a global understanding of the sphere of humane literacy. What is also at stake is redeeming the academy itself from some of the long-unresolved tensions in its own history, from some of its own recent and introverted preoccupation with theory—and thereby from the scorn it has earned, often justifiably, in the eyes of a skeptical public that yearns for help in living amid the complexities of our increasingly *American-and-Asian* world.

Asian Studies and Liberal Arts Colleges

A large part of the genius of American higher education, much appreciated through all its turmoil, is its diversity. Nowhere on earth, it has often been noted, have so many institutions with so many different missions, public and private, flourished in such diverse ways. This is true of American educational institutions as a whole, but it is also true of that special species of institution, the liberal arts college that is the central focus of this volume. In their original vision for this volume, the authors hoped to explore in some detail a range of examples of successful Asian studies programs. But in the discussions that led up to the writing of the several chapters and in reviewing the relevant evidence, it became apparent that the uniqueness of local factors and of institutional mission was often more decisive in launching Asian studies programs than the nature of Asian studies itself. Just as there is no one exclusive model for a successful liberal arts curriculum, so there is no one way that Asian studies should be brought into the liberal arts college. Consequently, this section focuses on some recurrent issues in bringing Asian studies into college life, noting several of the fundamental choices that faculty and administrators face in deciding what is appropriate for their particular campuses.

Our starting point must be to think of Asian studies in relationship to the related aspiration to internationalize the college curriculum. The former is not simply a subset of the latter, because of the unique place of Asia in human history and in the contemporary world, as noted earlier. There are two reasons, however, for emphasizing the convergence of Asian studies with international studies. First, there is today a decreasing legitimacy to thinking of any area of the world as autonomous. Each must be seen as part of the global whole. Second, the practice of "coalition building" is well advised in undertaking institutional change, and much that we know about internationalizing the curriculum can also be applied to "Asianizing" it. We turn therefore to a recent review by the Association of American Colleges and Universities (AAC&U) of strategies for "internationalizing the curriculum" and urge that its results be filtered through two lenses.[31] The first is Asia's uniqueness, underscored above, where ongoing consultation with Asia specialists can help shape appropriate conclusions. The second is the particular local campus culture with which the reader may be familiar.

We note, first, the caveat with which the authors of the AAC&U report introduce their survey. "Acquiring an international perspective," they warn, is not a "unitary concept" but covers "three quite distinctive kinds of learning: *knowledge* (a student's grasp of facts about international events), *affect* (attitudes and values about other peoples), and *language* (foreign language ability and attitudes toward foreign language study)."[32] Answering the question "What are our institution's goals for Asian studies?" is therefore the fundamental starting point for everyone wishing to undertake these initiatives. Discussion by interested parties and clarification of institutional mission are critical to success. This is not to say that exploration of multiple possibilities is not a viable strategy, nor that strategies cannot change based upon what an institution learns as the strategies unfold. It is to say that strategic planning is as critical here as it is elsewhere in college life.

The AAC&U survey then reports eleven kinds of initiative, which apply in varying ways to the range of possible goals for internationalizing or Asianizing the curriculum.[33] They are as follows:

1. Develop one course that draws on existing faculty expertise.
2. Offer language study across the curriculum.
3. Develop an intensive foreign language study program.
4. Add a new dimension—and coherence—to an existing set of courses through a "region across the curriculum" approach.
5. Combine study abroad with service abroad.
6. Focus on groups usually underrepresented in study-abroad populations.
7. Create the capacity for internationalizing courses by further developing the faculty.
8. Target professional education for internationalization and arrange for international internship placements.
9. Identify and use local community resources to enhance and complement efforts to internationalize.
10. Organize general education program around an international theme.
11. Make use of educational technology.

Several of these possibilities have obvious implications for increasing the presence of Asia in our colleges and call for little elaboration, and some will be explored in subsequent chapters. Here let me elaborate on four issues that are implicitly present in these strategies.

First, the question of whether to establish an autonomous Asian studies program or to infuse Asian studies throughout the curriculum is a basic one, to which there is no one "correct" answer. The conception and institutionalization of gender studies and women's studies programs over the past thirty years provide an instructive parallel. There is not a discipline in the humanities and social sciences that does not bear evidence of the fundamental and transformative effect that the study of gender has had on the academy. But has this made superfluous the need for interdisciplinary programs, where the study of gender is not at risk of being overwhelmed by more traditional disciplinary and departmental concerns? One suspects not, although this is a matter on which opinions—and political stances—vary enormously. There is no simple either-or solution. So, too, with regard to Asian studies. As one takes the long view of the academy's history, the rise and fall of disciplines makes a fascinating story. Where, for instance, were the social sciences a mere century ago? How an institution chooses to draw Asian studies into its institutional life will significantly be a function of how it chooses to accommodate the transformation that Asian studies will, in one way or another, effect on the academy's current disciplinary structure. Infusion and autonomy of program are the two foci of the ellipse.

A second and related issue pertains to the role of Asian studies specialists, on the one hand, and faculty who have developed a secondary interest and competence in Asian studies, while remaining rooted in other departments and disciplines, on the other. This, too, is a much contested area. Ainslie Embree notes in chapter six the debate at Columbia University when the prospect of an Asian humanities course emerged to complement the well-established Western Contemporary Civilization course. "How could those without training in the relevant languages teach on the basis of English translations?" cried the skeptics. The course nonetheless went forward, and the anthologies it produced—*Sources of Indian Tradition*, *Sources of Japanese Tradition*, and *Sources of Chinese Tradition*—have become indispensable to both students and teachers of Asia.[34]

Skeptical voices are still heard, of course, but they are not as shrill. One of the reasons for this is the manifest success of faculty development programs in enabling nonspecialists to turn their disciplinary expertise to Asian subject matter in ways that make sense to their own professional growth. ASIANetwork's Ford Foundation–funded Faculty Curricular Development Seminars on Japan, China, South Asia, and Southeast Asia and the Japan Seminar run by the AAC&U are only the most visible of these faculty development programs. Countless others exist, funded by sources both external and internal to individual colleges.

A further reason for the increasing convergence of purpose between Asian specialists and their nonspecialist colleagues may—and should— lie in our growing awareness of the absence of a significant correlation between scholarly research and teaching effectiveness in *any* field. Although this remains counterintuitive for many, and may even be considered anathema in many settings, a balanced review of the literature shows that "on average, there is a very small positive association between . . . research productivity or scholarly accomplishment of faculty members and their teaching effectiveness."[35] Similarly, if we look at the evidence specifically from a liberal arts college setting, the authors of a study conducted at Franklin and Marshall conclude by noting that while "there are many reasons why a small college might want to encourage its faculty to pursue scholarly research and publication, . . . it is unclear whether scholarly research and publication contribute at all to teaching and quite clear that they do not contribute much."[36] Correspondingly, while a college might want to insist on the presence of Asian studies specialists in order to mount a major or in the teaching of languages, it is clear that great strides can be made through the cultivation of Asian studies competence in faculty whose intellectual roots lie elsewhere. Once again, the notion of there being two complementary emphases, specialist and nonspecialist, two foci, proves useful.

A third issue worth noting is the increasing number of Asian studies faculty who are themselves Asians, born and trained in institutions far from America. While we earlier noted Anthony Reid's attack on Western intellectuals' preoccupation with theory at the expense of deep knowledge of area studies, the fact is that theory is no longer the property of the West. Some of the most stimulating and provocative work today— one thinks, for instance, of Edward Said's classic manifesto, *Orientalism*, or the emergence of "subaltern studies" in South Asia—is significantly an indigenous growth, a challenge to Western theorizing about Asia. This is, of course, very much what Wilfred Smith had in mind when he spoke of the corrective that Asian studies provides to longstanding assumptions in the academy. It is also very much what the Ford Foundation has wished to nurture with its above-noted crossing-borders call for "a more truly international area studies in which scholars . . . from diverse 'areas' shape the agenda and formulate, from their own perspectives . . . [what are the] important questions."[37] There is, of course, considerable peril here, as well as promise, for the importance of taking Asian scholarly perspectives seriously can slide easily into the politically charged claim that only Asians are qualified to articulate such perspectives. Here, as with other efforts to draw traditionally marginalized voices into the academy, the specter and the charge and the appearance of "political correctness" loom. As elsewhere, skilled leadership and open communication can ensure that the promise, rather than its alternative, is realized. Asianists who are Asian and those who are not again form a complementary pair.

Finally, one of the unique features of most liberal arts colleges is their residential character. People who live together learn from one another in powerful and unique ways. We have known this for a long time, but are only beginning to understand the issues analytically. The extension of this awareness into Asian studies cuts in two directions. For students and faculty who study in Asia, homestays—living with Asian families—are a critical ingredient, as Stephen Nussbaum explores in chapter four. But if we are to learn optimally from one another, we must realize that the movement of students in the *other* direction is of even greater potential. Of American students who study abroad, only 5 percent study in Asia. But nearly 450,000 foreign students have enrolled in American institutions since 1990, "a cohort about six times as large as that of U.S. students studying abroad." Of this huge cohort, nearly 60 percent come from Asia.[38] What, we may ask, are we doing to maximize the learning potential for all parties that exist when Asian students are in residence on our campuses? The possibilities here are enormous. The growing literature on "learning communities" can provide a useful starting point for exploring them.[39] Here, as elsewhere, a dialectical model of learning, one that emphasizes the relationship between the knower and what is known—more appropriately recast as the relationship between the knower and *those who* are known—may prove useful in expanding opportunities for Asian studies in liberal arts colleges, to the mutual enrichment of both.

Notes

1. Thorstein Veblen, *The Higher Learning in America*, 24–25.
2. W.B. Carnochan, *The Battleground of the Curriculum*, 22.
3. Ibid., 70.
4. Ibid., 86.
5. Ibid., 22.
6. Here I call "liberal arts colleges" those that the 1994 Carnegie classification defines as Baccalaureate (Liberal Arts) Colleges I. These are primarily undergraduate colleges with major emphasis on baccalaureate degree programs, selective in admissions, awarding more than 40 percent of their baccalaureate degrees in liberal arts fields. On the production of doctoral degrees, see *Baccalaureate Origins of Doctoral Recipients*. For a broader and very stimulating examination of liberal arts colleges today, see the essays in *Distinctively American*, a thematic issue of *Daedalus*.
7. International Liberal Arts Colleges, *In the International Interest*, 31, 26.
8. William Butler Yeats, "The Second Coming": "Turning and turning in the widening gyre / The falcon cannot hear the falconer; / Things fall apart; the centre cannot hold / Mere anarchy is loosed upon the world, / The dimmed tide is loosed, and everywhere / The ceremony of innocence is drowned; / The best lack all conviction, while the worst/Are full of passionate intensity" (W.B. Yeats, *The Poems*, 187).
9. In Thomas B. Coburn, "Nattering Nabobs, Habits of Mind, Persons in Relation," I have argued that "no particular subject matter is either intrinsically appropriate, or intrinsically inappropriate, to liberal arts study. It all depends on the intent with which it is studied, on whether it is subjected to the critical, wide-ranging inquiry that is the hallmark of this habit of mind." I then have gone on to suggest that even the study of motorcycles—if done with the relentless spirit of inquiry and

analysis that characterizes Robert Pirsig's *Zen and the Art of Motorcycle Mainte-nance*—potentially can find a place in the liberal arts curriculum. That Pirsig was so profoundly and creatively influenced by the Asian traditions of Daoism and Zen Buddhism makes the larger point of this chapter quite splendidly. For further stimu-lating development of a dynamic understanding of liberal education, past and present, see Martha Nussbaum, *Cultivating Humanity.*

10. Elizabeth Blake, "The Yin and Yang of Student Learning in College."

11. Thomas B. Coburn, "Cultural Memory and Postmodernism: A Pedagogical Note on Asian Studies." Rita Kipp makes a similar point in chapter five, where she urges us to help our students "understand cultures as sets of arguments, arenas of dispute," rather than "as little boxes inside which things are uniformly shared" (108).

12. This is the title of an essay in Jonathan Z. Smith, *Imagining Religion*, 19–35, but its theoretical emphasis on the epistemological centrality of comparison and the taxonomies it generates runs throughout the work that Smith does as both historian of religion and public intellectual.

13. Richard Perry, in commenting on a draft of this chapter, suggested that the traditional and postmodern critiques of particularity and parochialism carry quite different valances. The former, he suggested, produces a momentum toward engag-ing "the other" and seeks commonality as well as difference. The latter, by contrast, is mostly reflexive and invites students primarily to reflect on themselves, rather than on "the other." While this formulation may understate the continuity between the two positions, I am indebted to Professor Perry for suggesting this interesting and provocative distinction.

14. William B. Perry, Jr., *Forms of Intellectual and Ethical Development in the College Years.*

15. See Edmund Leach, *Claude Levi-Strauss*, 31–32.

16. Daryl G. Smith et al., *Diversity Works*, v–vii.

17. Ainslie T. Embree and Carol Gluck, eds., *Asia in World and Western History: A Guide for Teaching*, xviii.

18. For an overview of Project Kaleidoscope's work, see Web site *http://www.pkal.org*, which includes this general description: "Project Kaleidoscope (PKAL) is an informal national alliance of individuals, institutions, and organiza-tions committed to strengthening undergraduate science, mathematics, and technol-ogy education."

19. Myron L. Cohen, ed. The other two volumes in this project are the Embree and Gluck volume cited in note 17 and Barbara Stoler Miller, ed., *Masterworks of Asian Literature in Comparative Perspective.*

20. Rhoads Murphey, "The Shape of the World: Eurasia," in Embree and Gluck, *Asia in World and Western History*, 7.

21. Stanley O'Connor, "Humane Literacy and Southeast Asian Art," 147. I am indebted to Rita Kipp for introducing me to this phrase, which she also engages in chapter five (113, 121).

22. Arthur F. Wright, *Buddhism in Chinese History*, 33–34.

23. Ford Foundation, *Crossing Borders*, xii.

24. Ibid., v.

25. Diana Eck and the Pluralism Project at Harvard University, *On Common Ground.*

26. William Cantwell Smith, "The Role of Asian Studies in the American Uni-

versity." This address subsequently was printed and distributed by the Fund for the Study of the Great Religions of the World, Colgate University. I here take the liberty of substituting ungendered pronouns for the gendered usage that was common when Smith's talk was first delivered, a substitution that comes with his approval and is consistent with his own later usage.

27. Ibid., 2, 3.

28. Ibid., 3, 4, 5.

29. Ibid., 10.

30. Anthony Reid, "Studying 'Asia' Internationally," 53.

31. Joseph S. Johnston, Jr., and Jane R. Spalding, "Internationalizing the Curriculum," 416–35.

32. Ibid., 426.

33. I here cite in summary form the brief discussion and exemplification found in ibid., 426–34.

34. William Theodore de Bary is general editor of all three original *Sources* books, published first in 1958 and 1960. The Indian *Sources* appeared in a second edition in 1988. The Chinese *Sources* is in a second edition as of 1999 (vol. 1) and 2000 (vol. 2). The Japanese *Sources* is scheduled for a second edition in 2001.

35. Kenneth A. Feldman, "Research Productivity and Scholarly Accomplishment of College Teachers as Related to Their Instructional Effectiveness," 227.

36. Stanley J. Michalak, Jr., and Robert J. Friedrich, "Research Productivity and Teaching Effectiveness in a Small Liberal Arts College," 596. This study is based on a narrower definition of "scholarship" than that subsequently espoused by Ernest Boyer in *Scholarship Reconsidered: Priorities of the Professoriate*; but in light of the persistence of the narrower definition in the academy, somewhat mitigated in liberal arts colleges, these findings remain highly germane to our discussion. This complex issue recently has received sophisticated new attention in the important work of Alexander Astin, nicely summarized in his "How the Liberal Arts College Affects Students."

37. Ford Foundation, *Crossing Borders*, xii.

38. Johnston and Spalding, "Internationalizing the Curriculum," 420–21.

39. See Roberta S. Matthews, Barbara Leigh Smith, Jean MacGregor, and Faith Gabelnick, "Creating Learning Communities."

2

Asian Studies at American Private Colleges, 1808–1990

Samuel Hideo Yamashita

As the twenty-first century begins, Asia is a presence at most private colleges in the United States, with nearly every college offering courses on Asia. One hundred and forty-seven of the 154 colleges in the 1994 Carnegie listing of selection, category I liberal arts colleges have either courses on Asian subjects or Asian language instruction. Most of these colleges also give their students opportunities to live and study in Asia, as Stephen Nussbaum documents in chapter four. Ninety colleges teach one or more Asian languages, usually Japanese or Chinese but also Korean, Arabic, or South Asian languages, as Stanley Mickel observes in chapter three. Most remarkable, 76 colleges have a concentration in Asian studies or the equivalent, and 4 have minors. What makes this so impressive is that it took almost exactly two centuries for it to happen.

How courses on Asia came to be taught, faculty hired or retrained to teach Asian material, and Asian studies programs created is a complicated story, for the history of Asian studies at private colleges is really three intertwined stories. The first is the story of an evolving spiritual vision that brought "Asia" to these colleges in the nineteenth century; the second is the story of the American rediscovery of Asia before and during World War II and the postwar development of the Asian studies fields; and the third is the story of how private colleges, led by farsighted administrators and faculty and with support from charitable foundations, federal and state governments, private donors, and alumni, came to create Asian studies programs.

Thus "Asia" has existed in several different guises at private colleges. For all the nineteenth century and even into the twentieth, it was a "heathen" region in need of spiritual succor; in the middle years of the twentieth century, it was the subject of an occasional course, typically taught by a nonspecialist; and since the 1970s it has become a staple of many curricula and has greatly enriched the general education offerings of many colleges. All this confirms the metamorphosis that Asian studies has undergone at these institutions as the educational vision of administrators, faculty, and external donors changed and American commercial and geopolitical interests shifted.

Saving Asia (1808–1930)

Asia was part of a spiritual vision that first appeared on American college and university campuses in the early 1800s, long before courses on Asian subjects were first offered and students could major in Asian studies. In September 1808, Christian students at Williams College, led by young Samuel Mills, Jr., organized the Society of Brethren "to effect in the person of its members a mission to the heathen." Mills then carried his vision to Yale University and later to Andover Theological Seminary, where he organized the Society of Inquiry on the Subject of Missions. In June 1810, Mills and his followers petitioned the General Association of Congregational Churches in Massachusetts to establish foreign missions. The General Association responded by forming a "board of commissioners for foreign missions" to provide "missions for promoting the spread of the Gospel in heathen lands." During the next several years, students from both groups were sent on missions to India, Ceylon, and Africa.[1]

This was only the beginning. Religious societies appeared at nearly a dozen colleges over the next several decades—at Union, Amherst, Colby, Lafayette, Colgate, Gettysburg, Kenyon, Marietta, Bucknell, and Beloit—and large numbers of students signed up to spread the Word. In 1834, for example, the Missionary Lyceum of Wesleyan University was organized for "the benefit of the missionary cause," and a year later China was selected as the next "missionary field." Moses White '45 was the first Wesleyan student to serve in China, and he was followed by Erasmus Wentworth '37 and Marcus Lorenzo Taft '73.[2] By 1870, several hundred students from private colleges had been sent abroad, many to Asia.[3]

Students' interest in foreign missions is not surprising, given Christianity's formidable presence on college campuses in the nineteenth century. Indeed, most private colleges were founded by Christian educators, and most of their presidents and many of their faculty were clergymen. For example, all the faculty at Lafayette College in 1841 and half the faculty at Union College between 1795 and 1884 were ordained. As a result, most college administrators and faculty tried to instill the Christian concept of service in their students. "It always ought to be remembered," wrote Joseph McKeen, president of Bowdoin College, in 1804, "that literary institutions are founded and endowed for the common good, and not for the private advantage of those who resort to them for education." [4] In fact, the educational mission of these colleges was fundamentally Christian, and administrators and faculty sought not only to instill in their students Christian values but also to educate them for the ministry. [5]

In the mid-1800s, the impulse to serve assumed two new forms. A "home missionary movement," as it was called, impelled Christian educators to move westward and led to the founding of a half-dozen colleges in the West—Oberlin, Carleton, Grinnell, Colorado, Whitman, and Pomona. [6] The appearance of chapters of the Young Men's Christian Association (YMCA) and the Young Women's Christian Association (YWCA) on college and university campuses was another important development. The first chapters were founded at the University of Michigan and the University of Virginia, and new chapters opened at many other universities and colleges. By 1875, 17 private colleges had chapters. Since the YMCA and YWCA were an outgrowth of earlier Christian groups such as the Society of Brethren, they too sent willing students on overseas missions, and 2,100 students had "pledged to become heralds of the cross in any clime under the sun" by 1887. [7]

The missionary impulse was especially strong at private colleges, and a steady stream of students went off to Asia following graduation. Oberlin sent its first cohort to China in 1881. [8] In 1887, 6 of Carleton's 22 graduating seniors pledged "to spread the gospel in foreign lands," and ten years later 19 of its graduates were serving overseas as missionaries or teachers. Carleton, and later Grinnell and Oberlin, even established their own missions in China. In the fall of 1903, Carleton opened the Carleton Mission in China, which survived until 1948. [9] Oberlin started its Shansi program in 1908, and Grinnell founded its Grinnell-in-China program at Techow in Shantung in 1913. [10] A.B. Deltaan '06, who was already in China when the Grinnell program was proposed, wrote, "What we have in mind is to affiliate the educational work [here] directly with Grinnell." The college's commitment was amply represented in the size of its compound in Techow, which consisted of two hospitals, two middle schools, dormitories, and five mission houses.[11] In 1914, 6 Colorado College alumni were doing mission work abroad—3 in Persia, 2 in China and Korea, and 1 in India and Japan. In the 1920s, three Wesleyan University alumni were prominent Christian educators in China—John Gowdy '87 served as president of Fukien Christian University in Fuchou from 1923 to 1927, Joseph Beech '99 was the first president of West China Union University in Chengtu, and Edwin Jones '04 was president of Fukien Christian when he died in 1924.[12] Clearly, the impulse to serve overseas survived at these colleges well into the twentieth century.

Other developments in the United States also encouraged the missionary impulse. In the late nineteenth century and the early twentieth, as Progressivism swept the country, the idea of serving others caught on as what one commentator described as "a kind of middle-class sense of obligation, a readiness to bring American society to some new sense of its problems and promises."[13] America's emergence as an industrial and global power inspired confidence and optimism as well. American arms manufacturers in Springfield, Massachusetts, invented what came to be known as the "American system of manufacture," a method of mass production that Samuel Colt demonstrated at the Great Exhibition of 1851 when he took apart two six-shooters, mixed up their parts, and reassembled them. Organized along these lines, American factories produced everything from cotton goods to six-shooters both efficiently and cheaply.[14] When American products saturated the domestic market, manufacturers began to look overseas. Their search for foreign markets coincided with the country's rather sudden rise as an imperial power in 1898, when it annexed the Hawaiian Islands and acquired Spain's colonies in the Caribbean and Pacific.[15] Around this time, the first Asian students, mostly Japanese and Chinese, appeared on college campuses. Besides being one of the most famous, Jō Niijima (1843–1890), a young Japanese samurai, was surely the first from Japan. Apparently Niijima was so intrigued by Chinese translations of the Bible and Elijah Coleman Bridgman's *Historical Geography of the U.S.A.*, written in Chinese, that he stowed away on an American ship in 1864 and appeared at Amherst College in 1866.[16] He was the first of many Japanese to study at Amherst. Tsune Watanabe, a native of Kōbe, Japan, entered Carleton in 1888, majored in English, and was graduated in 1891. Carleton had at least one and possibly two other students from Japan in the 1890s, and these were part of a contingent of 12 foreign students at the college.[17] Oberlin had some Chinese students in the late 1800s, and Earlham nearly always had at least one Japanese student on campus from 1890 into the 1930s, usually a graduate of the Tokyo Friends School.[18] Wesleyan had a student from Japan named Ayskeh [sic] Kabayama, who was graduated in 1889 and went into business after returning home, eventually becoming the chairman of Japan Steel Works and a member of the House of Peers.[19] Nagai Kafū (1879–1959), a Japanese writer and admirer of the French naturalist novel, spent a semester studying French at Kalamazoo College in 1905 before he left for the East Coast and, eventually, Paris.[20] Colorado College had enough Chinese students in the mid-1920s that they formed their own social club.[21] In 1924 Amherst agreed to train young Japanese diplomats, as Carleton also did later.[22]

Growing numbers of missionary children also began to attend colleges with a strong denominational affiliation. Although they were American citizens, most had been raised overseas. Gordon Enders, a 1918 graduate of the College of Wooster, recalled that there were 50 missionary kids when he was there:

> Not a single one of the fifty had less than two languages; some of them spoke a half-dozen strange tongues and dialects. All of them had lived in far-off lands where strange adventures were commonplace. I was immediately thrown into fast growing friendships with youths from China, Korea, Persia, Japan, Syria, Indo-China, and Manchuria. My Asiatic background, hitherto confined almost entirely to Northern India and Tibet, began to fill in with a detailed picture of the peoples and problems of all other parts of that vast continent.[23]

Over meals in the dining halls, the missionary students discussed current Asian events, argued about the cultures of the countries where they grew up, and shared much-embellished tales of hair-raising treks and narrow escapes. They, too, brought Asia to campus.

These deepening ties with Asia must have pleased the administrators, faculty, and students at these colleges, for many had served in Asia as missionaries or educators. Charles Edmunds had been the president of Canton Christian College (later Lingnan University) from 1907 to 1924 before he became president of Pomona College in 1928, and his wife was raised in Sendai, Japan.[24] Others were active with the American Board of Commissioners for Foreign Missions, and a few had grown up in missionary homes in Asia and were sent to colleges with a firm Christian commitment to helping Asia, among them Carleton, Grinnell, Oberlin, and Wesleyan. Thus, the idea of saving Asia was still very much a concern at private colleges early in the twentieth century and survived until the late 1940s.

Rediscovering Asia (1930–1945)

Despite the growing Asian presence on college campuses, courses on Asian subjects were still a rarity in the first part of the twentieth century. A few big universities had offered courses on "oriental languages" since the mid-1800s, but because small colleges were more conservative, they were slow to follow the lead of the universities.

There were exceptions, however. In 1913 Francis Harding White, a Pomona College faculty member, offered Modern Asiatic History, a course described as "a study of the later life and institutions, chiefly of China and Japan; the changes under western influence and the various relations of Asia with America and Europe." White taught the course from 1913 to 1917.[25] In 1914 Kenneth Scott Latourette, recuperating from an illness contracted in China, was hired by Reed College to teach a course on the Far East.[26] That same year, a member of Wesleyan's history department taught a survey of constitutional government that had sections on India, China, and Japan.[27] Several other colleges followed suit. In 1916 Denison University hired Latourette, who had not been happy at Reed, and he remained there until 1921, when Yale lured him away.[28] In 1922 both Carleton and Wittenberg offered a course called The Far East.[29] In 1927 Whitman College began to offer a comparable course.[30] Two courses on Asia were given at Oberlin College while Edwin Reischauer was a student there in the late 1920s: Problems of the Pacific was taught by a nonspecialist and was "very superficial." An English scholar at Oberlin's school of theology taught a course on Mughal India, but Reischauer found his lectures filled with an unbearable amount of detail.[31] In 1930 Colorado College hired Carroll Malone, who had taught briefly at Tsinghua University in Peking, and he began to offer courses on Asian history. At St. Olaf College, former missionary John Bly taught a two-semester survey of Chinese and Japanese history beginning in 1937, and Amherst offered its first course on Asia, The Far East, in 1944.[32] These first courses show that the study of Asia was nearly nonexistent at private colleges in the first third of the twentieth century. Only a very small number of colleges offered such courses even sporadically, and they usually were taught by faculty with no specialized training in the Asian field.

In fact, only a handful of American scholars with a specialized knowledge of Asia were teaching anywhere in the United States in the early 1900s. Although the founding of the American Oriental Society in 1842 is said to mark the beginning of the formal study of Asia in this country, this group was organized "for the cultivation of learning in the Asian, African, and Polynesian languages" and had rather narrow philological interests.[33] Yale University began to offer Chinese language courses in 1877, the University of California at Berkeley created the Department of Oriental Languages in 1896, and in 1906 Stanford University hired Payson Treat, a Wesleyan graduate, to teach Far Eastern history.[34] As of 1914, only 8 universities had faculty who taught courses on Asia—Yale, Berkeley, Stanford, Harvard, Clark, Columbia, Wisconsin, and Washington. Although modest, these courses on Asia were the first sign that the study of Asia was being separated from Christianity.[35]

A surprisingly large number of doctoral dissertations on Asian subjects were written at American universities in the late 1800s, but their authors were foreign nationals—mostly Japanese—who appear to have returned to teach or work in their home countries.[36] At this time, most universities and nearly all private colleges simply did not include Asia in their curricula, despite the "academic revolution" then taking place, ushering in the elective system and naturalizing the German ideal of a research university. Perhaps it was a third innovation—a new curricular conception called "liberal education" or "general education" which focused on Western civilization—that ensured the exclusion of Asia from university and college curricula.[37]

Asia did not become part of college curricula until after World War II, and before that could happen, Asia had to be rediscovered, this time as an object of academic inquiry. The process began in earnest in the 1920s when private foundations, particularly the Rockefeller Foundation, began to fund Asian projects. The Rockefellers had long been interested in China. In 1909 John D. Rockefeller formed the Oriental Education Commission, which looked into China's contemporary situation and concluded that medicine was the area that most needed attention. Over the next forty years, the Rockefellers contributed $44,944,665 to this cause. The building and staffing of Peking Union Medical College, for example, was entirely funded by the Rockefellers, and in the late 1920s the foundation underwrote paleontological research in China.[38]

In the 1920s and 1930s, the Rockefeller Foundation and the American Council of Learned Societies gave money to individuals, groups, and institutions interested in studying Asia.[39] Several American scholars studying contemporary Asia at the graduate level received Rockefeller funds, including John King Fairbank, who was writing a doctoral dissertation on treaty ports in China at Oxford University, and Charles Burton Fahs, who was pursuing a doctorate in political science, with a specialization on Japan, at Northwestern University.[40] Fahs accepted a job at Pomona College in 1936 and chaired the newly created Department of Oriental studies, the first Asian studies program at a private college. He and two colleagues taught six courses on Asian topics: The Development of Oriental Civilization, History of Far Eastern Diplomacy, Contemporary Far Eastern Government, Political Problems of Eastern Asia, The Government of Japan, and Oriental Philosophy. They even gave a course in elementary Japanese, one of the earliest times an Asian language was offered at the college level.[41] Because the Rockefeller grant enabled Fahs to complete his doctorate, it is not surprising that Pomona's new Department of Oriental studies was created with Rockefeller money.

The Humanities Division of the Rockefeller Foundation also underwrote several summer institutes on contemporary Asia, one of which was held at Harvard in the spring of 1932.[42] Then another was held in the summer of 1940, with Reischauer and Fahs responsible for Japan, Fairbank and Derk Bodde handling China, and Archibald Wenley from the Freer Gallery introducing the fine arts. Fairbank remembers the second institute as "a high-powered survey of history and bibliography aimed at a selection of a dozen young American teachers to start them off in preparation for teaching on East Asia."[43] The American Council of Learned Societies (ACLS) funded still another institute at Cornell in the summer of 1941.[44]

The Rockefeller Foundation funded three other projects that were important to the development of Asian studies in the United States. In 1933, working through ACLS, the foundation began to help build an Asian collection at the Library of Congress. The following year, the foundation, once again working through ACLS, funded summer language institutes that offered Chinese, Japanese, and Russian language courses at Harvard, Columbia, Cornell, and the University of California at Berkeley. By 1941, 12 universities offered one or more of these languages.[45] During World War II, these Rockefeller-funded language programs proved invaluable. David Stevens, head of Rockefeller's Division of Humanities, remembers that "the practical services rendered by the humanities division during the war were of vital importance and surprised many skeptics who had insisted on thinking of the humanities as a useless luxury."[46] Finally, Rockefeller money enabled the establishment of scholarly organizations devoted to the study of Asia, such as the Institute of Pacific Relations, founded in 1925, and the Far East Association, which met for the first time in June 1941.[47] Rockefeller support was indispensable to the rediscovery of Asia and the early development of Asian studies.

No single event encouraged the rediscovery of Asia more than World War II. First, the war moved the handful of newly trained Asian specialists away from the academy and into government. In the summer of 1941, for example, both John Fairbank and Edwin Reischauer left Harvard University for the Research and Analysis Section of the State Department, and in September Burton Fahs left Pomona "to handle Japan" in the same office.[48] Fairbank served with the Coordinator of Information, then with the Office of Strategic Services, before leaving for China, where he was special assistant to the U.S. ambassador. In 1944, he returned to the Office of War Information in Washington, D.C., and a year later assumed the post of director of the U.S. Information Service in China.[49] In 1942, Reischauer, who had returned to Harvard at the end of the summer, was asked to help the Army Signal Corps set up a school for translators and cryptologists in Washington, D.C. After returning briefly to Harvard, Reischauer moved to G-2, the intelligence section of the general staff, where, he reports, he analyzed the intelligence gleaned from intercepted Japanese messages. Following Japan's surrender, Reischauer moved once again to the State Department, where he helped formulate policy for the Allied Occupation of Japan.[50]

After the war ended, most of the Asia specialists serving in the government returned to their campuses. In the fall of 1946 Reischauer and Fairbank returned to Harvard, and Hugh Borton, a Japan specialist trained at the University of Leiden in the 1930s who spent the war at the State Department, took a position at Columbia University.[51] Others, however, stayed on in the government. Burton Fahs chose not to return to Pomona and eventually became the head of the Office of Intelligence and Research in the State Department, remaining in government until the 1950s.[52] The war had thus created a close relationship among government, private foundations, and the emerging community of Asia scholars. To specialists like John Fairbank, this was inevitable:

> The buildup of American research on China after 1945 was thus an act of national policy even though it was carried on mainly by the private sector

of foundations and universities. As we went ahead with our training and research at Harvard and other centers it became plain that we were creating a body of knowledge and a corps of teachers that the country needed.[53]

Asianists continued for some time to move easily among the academy, government, and private foundations. The most famous example was Edwin Reischauer, who left Harvard to become the U.S. ambassador to Japan in 1961 and returned to Harvard in 1966.[54]

The war's second effect on the Asian field was unexpected. The wartime demand for intelligence specialists, cryptologists, and translators led to the creation of several Chinese- and Japanese-language schools for military personnel. The Chinese schools were initially housed at the University of California at Berkeley and Harvard, and then at the University of Colorado, and the Japanese schools were ensconced at Colorado, the University of Michigan, and Camp Savage, Minnesota. All together, nearly 20,000 army and navy men, and a number of women as well, took the intensive course in Chinese and Japanese.[55]

Several dozen of the young men trained as interpreters and translators went on to do graduate work in Asian fields, which was a boon for Asian studies. Army Language School trainee Robert Brower, for example, did graduate work in classical Japanese literature at the University of Michigan and became an expert on classical Japanese poetry, later teaching at Stanford and Michigan. The Navy Language School at Colorado also produced several leading scholars: both Joseph Levenson and William Theodore deBary did graduate work in Chinese history and became leading Chinese intellectual historians.[56] Donald Keene and Edward Seidensticker became prominent translators of Japanese literature and almost singlehandedly introduced the best of Japanese literature to American readers. Warren Tsuneishi wrote a doctoral thesis at Yale on the Japanese emperor system and eventually became head of the Oriental Collection at the Library of Congress.[57] Two fine scholars emerged from Reischauer's Army Signal Corps School in Arlington, Virginia: Benjamin Schwartz wrote a thesis on Chinese communism before the revolution and became an intellectual historian of China, and Howard Hibbett wrote a thesis on eighteenth-century Japanese fiction and became a translator and critic. Both men earned their graduate degrees at Harvard and stayed on to teach there.[58] Hawaiian-born George Akita, a graduate of the Military Intelligence School at Camp Savage, Minnesota, did his graduate work at Harvard, where he wrote a thesis on the Meiji constitution, and taught at the University of Hawaii.[59] One commentator calculated that almost a quarter of the 695 graduate students enrolled in American doctoral programs in area studies in 1951 were veterans of World War II.[60] The war was good for Asian studies.

The prewar and war years (1930–1945) thus laid the foundation for Asian studies in the United States. With generous support from the Rockefeller Foundation and the guidance of the American Council of Learned Societies, new academic programs focused on Asia were created. The growing tension in Asia and worsening American relations with Japan led to a series of summer institutes on Asia, run by newly trained American Asia specialists. Later, the outbreak of war in the Pacific created a huge demand for Asia specialists, which was mostly met with crash courses in Japanese and Chinese. After the war, many of those trained in these programs did graduate work in Asian fields and continued the work of their predecessors. Asia had been rediscovered.

Studying Asia (1946–1960)

After World War II, more private colleges began to offer courses on Asian subjects, but the number was still small. In 1946 Macalester College began to give courses on East Asian history, and Colgate University listed The Far East in Modern Times.[61] Brooklyn College taught both a survey history of East Asia and Chinese language courses beginning in 1947.[62] The faculty at Skidmore College taught the college's first courses on Chinese literature and East Asian history, philosophy, religion, and art; Middlebury offered a course on Asian art; and a faculty member at the University of Puget Sound taught the History of the Far East.[63] All these courses seem to have been taught by faculty with no formal training in Asian studies.

Colleges also began to hire Asia specialists. Once again, Pomona may have been the first. After Burton Fahs left in 1941, the college hired a Chinese émigré named Ch'en Shou-yi, who had a doctorate in Oriental studies from the University of Chicago and considerable teaching experience at Peking University and the University of Hawaii.[64] In 1946, Pomona hired a second Asia specialist, Allan Cole, who had a Ph.D. in modern Japanese history from the University of Chicago. Over the next several years, Ch'en and Cole, with the help of several other colleagues, taught three years of Chinese and nearly a dozen courses on Asia.[65] Pomona, however, was the exception.

Most colleges began to hire Asia specialists in the 1950s. In 1950 Oberlin hired Ellsworth Carlson, a Chinese history specialist who had done his graduate work with Fairbank at Harvard and worked in the Office of Strategic Services and at the China desk at the State Department.[66] In 1958 Hamilton College hired Edwin Lee, a Japan specialist from Columbia who taught courses on Chinese and Japanese history. Lee's presence proved catalytic, and soon a colleague in the Department of Philosophy and Religion was offering Religions of the Far East.[67] That same year Wesleyan hired David Abosch, the first of several Japan specialists who taught there.[68] In 1959 Jackson Bailey, armed with a doctorate in Japanese history from Harvard, accepted a position at Earlham College and immediately began to build one of this country's first undergraduate Japanese studies programs.[69] In 1960 Amherst hired James Crowley, its first Asia specialist, who had just completed a thesis at the University of Michigan on Japanese factional politics in the 1930s. When he left for Yale, Amherst hired Paul Cohen, one of Fairbank's students from Harvard. When Cohen moved to Wellesley, Amherst found Ray Moore, who had studied Japanese history at Michigan. Moore stayed at Amherst and played a large part in the creation of Asian studies in the Amherst-Northampton area.[70]

Most colleges that offered courses on Asia still did so without Asia specialists. For example, beginning in the 1950s, Colgate had a full array of courses on Asia—in geography, history, religion, and art—all of which were taught by nonspecialists. These courses were apparently well received, as they enrolled around 5 percent of the student body.[71] Even those colleges that hired Asia specialists still relied on nonspecialists. Earlham, for example, had Jackson Bailey's courses, but it also offered courses on Japanese art, music, philosophy, and politics—all taught by nonspecialists.[72]

Many more colleges might have wanted to offer courses on Asia but could not for two reasons. First, faculty support was often lukewarm. Hyman Kublin, a newly hired Japanese history specialist at Brooklyn College, remembers that "the faculty has not found it difficult to accept *intellectually* the value of learning about alien cultures. But in the manner of college teachers everywhere, the response to the educational, and, much more, the curricular implications of this proposition has been lukewarm."[73] Second, financial resources were limited, especially at private colleges, and so the creation of new positions in Asian fields was virtually impossible.

The Asian studies initiative was kept alive at many colleges during the late 1940s and 1950s through a combination of administrative support, faculty leadership, and external funding. Brooklyn College was typical. Despite the tepid response of its faculty, the president and deans provided what Kublin described as "firm and unwavering support," which attracted a Rockefeller grant for a self-study of area studies programs at the college. A special presidential committee consisting of Brooklyn College's own area specialists resulted in four new courses, one of which was The Far East and India, a team-taught, two-semester survey of Asian history.[74]

In what were lean days for Asian studies at private colleges, foundation support provided the only hope. Consider what happened in Indiana in the late 1950s. Beginning in 1958, the American Council of Learned Societies and the Ford Foundation funded a statewide initiative in Indiana entitled "The Project for Extending the Study of Foreign Areas in Indiana Undergraduate Education." The "Indiana Project," as it was called, set out to broaden undergraduate education and

> to equip students to participate in a world very different from that which existed when present curricula and educational policies were established. Problems and discussions that must be faced in the next half century require an appreciation and understanding of the histories and aspirations of the societies of Africa and Asia.[75]

This ambitious project used several different methods to achieve these lofty goals but relied most heavily on faculty retraining. Selected faculty and administrators from Indiana colleges were sent to universities with area studies programs for intensive study of a non-Western area that lasted for a semester, a year, or even longer, and upon their return to their home campuses they offered new courses in that area. In 1960–1961, for example, Wendell Calkins, chair of the history department at Wabash College, studied Chinese and "Far Eastern Civilization" at a local university and then gave a course on that subject. Faculty seminars on specific areas were organized as well. In 1960–1961, Depauw University organized a seminar on Africa, and Marian College did the same for the Middle East. Periodic regional seminars were popular: a two-day seminar on Southeast Asia was cosponsored by eight colleges and held in Fort Wayne in September 1960, with 45 college faculty, students, and teachers attending.[76]

The Indiana Project's impact was mainly curricular, with the retrained faculty offering new courses on Asia or enriching existing ones upon their return to campus. Hanover College was typical. A faculty committee charged with revising the curriculum proposed that every junior study "East Asian civilization and some non-Western literature." The proposal was accepted by the entire faculty, and the former dean of the college was sent to Harvard to learn about East Asia. Then, when he returned to Hanover, he oversaw the creation and teaching of the new courses on Asia.[77]

The Indiana Project also revealed that faculty retraining might not be sufficient to introduce Asia into the curriculum. Writing in 1961, John Thompson, director of the project, expressed some dissatisfaction with the faculty-retraining approach and suggested that it serve only as an "interim measure." He admitted that he looked forward to "the addition to smaller college faculties of teachers trained to deal competently with different areas of the non-Western world." Thompson then offered a prescient observation about these Asia specialists. They "should be prepared, psychologically and professionally," he wrote, "to teach in the private colleges, being willing both to forgo excessive specialization in their area and to participate fully, willingly, and effectively in the basic disciplinary work that will continue to comprise the bulk of college departmental offerings."[78] He clearly anticipated three problems: the first was the relative paucity of American scholars with graduate training in Asian fields. The second was the reluctance of Asia specialists to teach at private colleges. The third was that many Asia specialists had extensive area studies training but less in particular disciplines. Thompson was right, as these were precisely the problems that administrators and faculty at private colleges faced when they attempted to expand their Asian curricula in the 1960s and 1970s.

Emerging Asian Fields (1960–1970)

Before these problems could be solved, much had to happen. First, more degree-awarding graduate programs had to be created, producing more Asia specialists. In 1946, only 4 major universities in the United States had full-blown Asian studies programs, all focused on China and Japan. By 1951, there were 11 such programs, representing a broader array of regions and countries: 8 concentrating on China and Japan (Columbia, Cornell, Harvard, Johns Hopkins, Michigan, University of California at Berkeley, University of Washington, and Yale); 2 directed to Southeast Asia (Cornell and Yale); and 1 devoted to South Asian studies (University of Pennsylvania).[79] In 1973, there were 76 programs—43 focused on East Asia, 20 on South Asia, and 13 on Southeast Asia.[80]

Each of these Asian studies programs required a team of faculty to teach a full range of courses on Asia, spanning several disciplines. The first cohort of faculty were the pioneers—Fairbank, Reischauer, Borton, Bodde, and others trained in the 1930s. The second consisted of the veterans of the military language schools, now out of uniform and holding doctorates. After them came those who had completed their dissertations in the 1950s and early 1960s. Each program also taught Asian vernacular languages, courses that were developed in the 1950s with the help of linguists and native speakers. By 1960 more than a dozen university programs offered Chinese; 9 offered Japanese; 3 offered one or more Southeast Asian languages; and 2 offered South Asian languages. Korean, Mongolian, and Tibetan also were taught, although not as a part of a complete Asian area studies program.[81]

What was emerging in the 1950s was an Asian studies field, or perhaps a series of fields, centering on China, Japan, South Asia, and Southeast Asia. As with all academic fields, there was competition for scarce resources, so methods for deciding who would receive these resources were necessary. One such method was the founding of scholarly organizations, which provided not only opportunities for scholarly contact and exchange but also a means for senior scholars to oversee the development of the new fields. The Far Eastern Association, founded in 1941, became an established scholarly organization in 1948, and as its membership grew steadily through the 1950s and exponentially in the 1960s it became the most powerful organization of its kind in the United States. Membership in the association grew dramatically in the 1950s and 1960s, from 606 in 1949 to 4,708 in 1970.[82]

Publication was a second method for managing the Asian studies fields. Academic journals in which Asia specialists could publish articles were needed. The Far Eastern Association put out the *Far Eastern Quarterly.* In addition, there were the *Journal of the American Oriental Society*, the *Harvard Journal of Asiatic Studies*, and the *Transactions of the Asiatic Society of Japan.*[83] When the Far Eastern Association changed its name to the Association for Asian Studies in 1956, its journal became the *Journal of Asian Studies.* The presses at the universities with Asian area studies programs helped, too, by publishing recently completed doctoral dissertations. Harvard University Press took the lead, publishing 151 books on East Asia between 1956 and 1976 (124 books on China,

23 on Japan, and 4 on Korea).[84] The presses at California, Columbia, Hawaii, Michigan, Princeton, Stanford, Washington, and Yale joined in the effort. In any case, the manuscript review process offered senior Asianists on editorial committees a means of establishing what was acceptable scholarly work and what was not, and the result was an authoritative (that is, authorized) body of knowledge about Asia.

The postwar Asian studies fields had another feature that cannot be overlooked: They were developed under the rubric of "area studies," an approach that focused "all the disciplinary competences (geography, history, economics, language and literature, philosophy, political science and the like) upon a cultural area for the purpose of obtaining a total picture of that culture."[85] This proved to be both a blessing and a curse. On the positive side, "area studies," although hardly monolithic, offered a useful conceptual language, or discourse, that faculty and students in different disciplines shared, a discourse that affirmed empirical, comparative, and multidisciplinary approaches. Area studies was also familiar, as it had first appeared in the 1930s and then reemerged during World War II "to train men for the two great theaters of operation, Europe and the Far East."[86] After the war, area studies survived as American interest in the non-Western world grew and new anthropological concepts of "culture" and cultural relativism supplied a means of organizing knowledge of non-Western peoples.[87]

The area studies programs that were established in the late 1940s through the 1950s were cursed, however, by their success, for there was no faculty consensus on the value of such programs at the universities where they emerged. In this respect, Asian area studies programs were quite different from other university-wide measures, such as curricular reform, that were formulated in faculty discussions before they became policy. Instead, area studies programs had a jerry-built quality. Indeed, it struck one careful observer that they required "entrepreneurship" rather than intellect.[88] A second problem was that as departments and disciplinary specialization gained new favor at American colleges and universities, "area studies" became an outdated educational concept.[89] The tension between traditional disciplines and area studies was apparent from the outset, and in the early 1970s the merits of the "area specialist" versus the "disciplinary generalist" were even debated, suggesting the suspicion with which area studies continued to be viewed in many quarters.[90] This should not be surprising, however, for "discipline takes precedence over area at the Ph.D. level," as John Hall put it so well. Finally, area studies programs were also somewhat isolated and peripheral at their home institutions, which prompted Hall to wonder whether they really had much impact on the students.[91] These problems were serious and even jeopardized university Asian studies programs.

Two events ensured the survival of Asian area studies. The first was the Cold War. The country desperately needed to know more about Asia, for both ideological and scholarly reasons.[92] Fairbank's elegant characterization of the Chinese studies field applies equally well to other Asian studies fields—their creation was "an act of national policy."[93] The Russians' successful launching of *Sputnik* in 1957 underscored the need to know more about those parts of the world where the United States and its allies were expected to do battle with the Soviet Union and its satellites, and Asia was high on that list. Throughout the 1950s and 1960s, the growing cadre of Asia specialists was as indispensable to the government as their precursors had been during World War II. Richard Lambert openly acknowledged the Asian studies community's ties with the government:

> The centers and their faculties provide a repository of expertise on which government can and does draw for research, consultation, or temporary employment. The graduate students produced at the centers are an important recruitment source for the foreign affairs agencies. Much of the literature which stocks international agency libraries is produced by individuals in these centers. The government also uses these centers for the training of current employees.[94]

The Vietnam War years revealed just how closely Asianists worked with federal agencies and how "strategic" the Asian studies fields had become.[95]

External funding also helped save Asian area studies programs. University administrators do not turn their back on major funders—or not easily, at least. A newly reorganized Ford Foundation was extraordinarily generous to area studies programs, donating $270 million between 1953 and 1966.[96] The other major funders were the Rockefeller and Luce Foundations, the Carnegie Corporation, and, after 1957, the federal government.[97] Although the foundations gave generously to the Chinese, Japanese, Southeast Asian, and South Asian fields, the Chinese field received the lion's share of the funding, owing to the strategic nature of knowledge about China. Not only was the People's Republic of China an ally of the Soviet Union, but also it had prevailed on the Chinese mainland in 1949 and sent troops to fight the Allies in the Korean War.

The federal government's contribution to the China field amounted to $15,040,000 between 1958 and 1970, and both public and private funding totaled $44,451,910 between 1946 and 1970.[98] The reason for the federal programs under the National Defense Education Act (NDEA), including National Defense Foreign Language (NDFL) fellowships, was clearly the strategic nature of knowledge about Asia. The country required more Asia specialists who could read vernacular languages and were familiar with contemporary Asian affairs. These external grants not only funded Asia area studies programs but also helped them get established on their home campuses in the 1950s and 1960s.

The Henry Luce Foundation deserves special mention. In the late 1960s, both Ford and federal money began to dry up, precipitating a crisis in the Asian studies field. Once flush with money, the major area studies programs now faced the prospect of greatly reduced budgets and thus smaller graduate programs. In 1974 the Luce Foundation, recognizing "that the American academic community finds itself in a growing financial pinch with respect to Asian studies," created the Luce Fund for Asian Studies and distributed $3 million to 12 major Asia centers at Chicago, Columbia, Cornell, Harvard, Michigan, Princeton, and Stanford, among others.

Luce gave generously to the Asian fields through the 1980s. In fact, in the late 1980s the foundation rescued the dying Southeast Asian studies field with a $5 million grant that was to be used for faculty development and library building. Once again, the four leading Southeast Asian studies centers received funds—Cornell, Northern Illinois, Wisconsin, and Yale.[99]

Asian studies thus owes much to the Cold War. The threat of an impending East-West conflict reaffirmed the strategic value of the concept of area studies, and it was used to organize the many programs focused on Asia and other parts of the world that emerged at major universities in the postwar period. Asia programs proliferated in the 1950s and 1960s, increasing from 4 to 76 in just over two decades, thanks to the millions of dollars they received from charitable foundations and the federal government in the name of both national security and scholarship. Although the success of these programs troubled some and raised important educational questions, the programs did represent, for better or worse, the establishment of the several Asian studies fields in this country.

Asian Studies at Private Colleges (1960–1990)

The emergence of these Asian studies fields in the 1950s and 1960s had important consequences for private colleges. More than 2,000 doctoral dissertations on Asian subjects had been completed at American universities between 1960 and 1969, and so more Asia specialists were now available. Although most took jobs at universities or in government agencies, a few went to private colleges. The latter, having been trained at major area studies programs, were well equipped to take the lead in creating Asian studies programs.

The new faculty members were mostly historians, perhaps because history was one of the core disciplines of area studies and there were simply more new Ph.D.'s in history. Hiring Asia historians at this time were Wesleyan (1958), Earlham (1959), Hamilton (1959), Amherst (1960), Carleton (1964), Wittenberg (1967), Macalester (1968), Whitman (1969), Connecticut (1970), and the University of Puget Sound (1971). Other colleges hired scholars with training in other fields. St. Lawrence brought aboard a Thai politics expert in 1971, Middlebury hired a Chinese linguist in 1976, St. Olaf found a Buddhist specialist in 1977, and some colleges hired anthropologists or sociologists.[100] Asian literature specialists were usually hired after social scientists, perhaps because they were needed mainly to teach language, and most colleges did not decide to offer Asian languages until the late 1970s. But literature specialists were in great demand in the 1980s as Japanese-language study spread. From the vantage point of 2000, an Asian studies program without Asian literature specialists is inconceivable.

The 1960s also proved to be a period of adjustment for many new Asian studies programs. Many Asianists found that they were not satisfied with undergraduate teaching and left for bigger institutions with graduate programs. Both Amherst and Carleton, for example, lost Japan historians to major research universities in the 1960s, and they were not unusual in this respect. Because Asian studies programs were just taking shape at many colleges in the 1960s, most still had only one or two Asianists and relied on the courses offered by nonspecialists. As the roster of Asianists grew, it became easier to hire others and to keep them.

More Asia specialists on the faculty meant more courses on Asia. Assuming that each new faculty member had departmental obligations as well, each brought in from 6 to 8 new courses with Asian content. Thus, a cohort of 3 or 4 Asianists meant 18 to 32 new courses on Asia, and a greater variety of courses as well. If the 1950s brought the first history courses on Asia taught by specialists, the mid-1960s and 1970s brought courses in political science, religion, anthropology, sociology, and occasionally literature and art history.

With growing numbers of Asianists and courses on Asia, concentrations in Asian studies or the equivalent became feasible. In the 1950s, only Colgate, Earlham, and Pomona had an Asian concentration, but the 1960s saw the establishment of more programs with an Asian studies concentration, including Skidmore (1961), Bucknell (1965), Oberlin (1965), Carleton (1966), Randolph Macon (1967), Claremont McKenna (1968), Pitzer (1968), St. Olaf (1968), and Vassar (1969). It was in the 1970s, however, that Asian studies programs proliferated: Connecticut and Wittenberg (1970), Hamilton and Hobart and William Smith (1972), Macalester and Puget Sound (1973), Amherst and Wesleyan (1974), and Washington and Lee (1978). This trend continued through the 1980s as more colleges decided to create Asian studies programs and hired faculty with Asian specialties. Colleges creating Asian studies concentrations in the 1980s included Mt. Holyoke (1980), Wellesley (1980), Grinnell (1985), Vassar (1985), St. Lawrence (1985), Bowdoin (1987), and Smith (1988). These new concentrations assumed different forms, depending on both the specialties of the new faculty members and local circumstances, and were variously called Asian, East Asian, Chinese, Japanese, or South Asian studies.

The 1970s and 1980s brought a number of new developments that transformed the study of Asia at private colleges. First, undergraduate teaching became more attractive to Asianists from the most highly regarded graduate programs. The growing number of area specialists created a tighter job market, and more new Ph.D.'s were willing to consider teaching at a private college.[101] The hiring of more Asia specialists also made the prospect of living in small and often remote college towns more palatable to young scholars who were from Asia or had just spent several years doing research there. Collegeville was no match for Beijing, Tokyo, or Chiang Mai. Thus, the expansion of Asian studies meant that the new faculty member would have colleagues with similar experiences and training, identical professional goals, and the same compelling need to spend part of every summer and sabbaticals in Asia.

No college proceeded more carefully than Carleton. In 1966, it established an Asian studies committee to plan the expansion of Asian studies at the college. "From the start the Asianists among us carefully planned how we wanted the program to grow," remembers Bardwell Smith, one of the architects of this expansion, "and all along the line we were in conversation with other colleagues in specific departments and with the key administrators (specifically, the president and dean of the college) and from time to time with interested trustees." Since the faculty already included specialists in East and South Asian religions and South Asian sociology and anthropology, the committee decided on an order of expansion that began with East Asian history, followed by one East Asian language, Japanese. Their next move was to hire a political scientist with Asian expertise, after which they added a second position in Japanese and two in Chinese. The Carleton group were as patient as they were careful, and it paid off.[102]

The 1980s found Asia specialists in greater demand, a second important development. Among the many reasons for this was the meteoric rise of the Asian economies. With Japan's emergence in 1985 as the world's greatest creditor nation and the subsequent rise of the "Asian Tigers"—South Korea, Taiwan, Hong Kong, Singapore, Thailand, and Malaysia—Asia demanded attention and so could not be left out of the college curriculum. Even economists, normally disdainful of area studies, expressed an interest in Asian studies.

The redefinition of general education in the late 1970s and early 1980s was a third development that greatly affected the fortunes of Asian studies at private colleges. There was movement in this direction as early as the 1960s. In 1962, for example, John Nason, the president of Carleton, called for a new kind of education that would equip students "to wrestle with the problems of cultural diversity."[103] William Pusey, dean at Washington and Lee and the author of a successful grant proposal that led to the creation of a Chinese studies program, recalls that "there seemed to be a gap in what we were offering."[104] It was in the 1970s, however, that some of these new conceptions of general education were integrated into the curriculum. Unlike those popular in the early 1900s, which focused on Western civilization, these new conceptions were typically not Eurocentric. One of the first was the "foreign cultures" requirement that the Harvard faculty adopted in 1978, which mandated that each student take a course dealing with a foreign culture "to expand the student's range of cultural experience and to provide fresh perspectives on the student's own cultural assumptions and traditions."[105] Because the Harvard requirement inspired faculty elsewhere to adopt similar requirements or to create programs and courses informed by the same spirit, scholars specializing in the non-Western world and their courses achieved new prominence.

Surely no one felt the need for curricular diversity more strongly than college presidents and deans. Working with interested faculty, administrators at nearly every private college in the country created new positions in Asian fields in the 1970s and 1980s. An unprecedented development, this expansion led to more than 80 colleges hiring one or more faculty with Asian specialties in the 1970s and 1980s, which in turn led to the creation of nearly 50 new Asian studies programs at private colleges.

During the 1970s, through the 1980s, and continuing into the 1990s, a number of colleges dramatically expanded their Asian programs. The University of Puget Sound, for example, added 7 new positions in Asian fields, and Whitman and Washington and Lee each added 6.[106] At Puget Sound, the advice of the late Jackson Bailey, architect of Earlham's outstanding Japanese studies program and the leading consultant on undergraduate Asian studies programs, was of critical importance. Puget Sound had several faculty with Asian interests, including a junior faculty member trained in Asian religions and a senior faculty member in the religion department who, though not an Asia specialist, was committed to Asian studies, and a newly hired China historian. Bailey, whose consultancy was brought in with grants from the National Endowment for the Humanities and the Lilly Foundation, helped faculty at Puget Sound "achieve . . . a new structure for the major, an understanding of how to incorporate language study with the major, an appreciation of the value of non-Asia trained colleagues . . . in expanding the curriculum of the program, and the prior importance of participating in the university's program of general education." Puget Sound created new or additional positions in South Asian anthropology (mid-1970s), Japanese language (1982), Asian comparative politics (early 1980s), Asian religions (1990s), Asian art history (early 1990s), Asian political economy (1990s), and Japanese literature and culture (1997).[107]

At Whitman, the collaboration of a China historian and a new president was crucial. Together they initiated the expansion, generating new positions in Japanese language and literature (1981), South Asian anthropology (1983), Japanese politics (1983), Chinese language and literature (1985), South Asian religions (1996), and Islam and the Middle East (1997). Although an Americanist by training, Whitman's president became an ardent supporter of Asian studies, made several trips to Asia, and worked hard "to open his institution up to the wider world, especially Asia."[108]

At Washington and Lee, in contrast, the leadership of deans was decisive in the development of Asian studies. A dean wrote successful grant proposals in the 1970s that funded library acquisitions, lectures and cultural events, and the retraining of two faculty—one studied Asian politics and the other studied Chinese philosophy. In the late 1970s, the Association of Chinese Artists and Writers of Taiwan and the Rotary Club of Taipei donated 1,000 books in Chinese for Washington and Lee's growing Asian collection, and in 1980 the college received a Japan Foundation Library Support Program grant. During the tenure of the succeeding dean, Washington and Lee was awarded two substantial Andrew W. Mellon Foundation grants that led to the creation of new positions in Asian economics, Japanese, and Chinese. These grants as well as internal monies funded a total of 6 new positions—in Japanese religion, Japanese history, Japanese economics, Japanese literature, and Japanese language—and teaching assistantships in both Chinese and Japanese.[109] The experiences of Puget Sound, Whitman, and Washington and Lee confirm once again the importance of administrative and faculty leadership when developing Asian studies programs. Without such leadership, success is difficult, if not impossible.

The expansion of Asian studies programs in the 1970s and 1980s had one other important ingredient, the availability of external funding. Several new foundations funded undergraduate institutions intent on expanding their cohort of Asia specialists. Of these, the Japan Foundation was by far the most generous. Between 1974 and 1995, it awarded staff expansion grants to 27 colleges, creating 34 new positions in Japanese fields, mostly in Japanese language and literature. The Chiang Ching-kuo Foundation, another new funding source, also underwrote a number of new positions in Chinese language and literature at private colleges.[110] The Freeman Foundation, based in Stowe, Vermont, was another new funder of Asian studies at the undergraduate level, giving generously first to Wesleyan and then in the 1990s to dozens of other colleges.[111]

The long-established foundations also helped the growth of Asian studies in private colleges. The Luce and Ford foundations, which had supported Asian area studies programs at the university level for several decades, turned their attention to private colleges in the 1970s and 1980s. Since then, Luce has donated more than $1,075,000 and Ford more than $739,100. The Fulbright commission in Tokyo helped several institutions start Japanese language instruction, for example, Amherst in 1970–1971 and St. Lawrence in 1986–1987. Federal funding contributed as well, with a 1975 NDEA Title VI grant making possible the creation of a five-college Asian studies program in the Amherst-Northampton area in Massachusetts. Grants from the Department of Education in the 1970s helped develop South Asian studies at Furman University, Guilford College, and St. Andrews Presbyterian College. National Endowment for the Humanities grants were awarded to Skidmore to rescue an ailing Asian studies program (1975–1977) and to Puget Sound for curricular development and faculty expansion (1977–1979). The Andrew W. Mellon Foundation gave generously to many institutions, including Washington and Lee.[112]

Private colleges have been helped also by regional foundations and generous donors. In the 1960s, Carleton received two major grants: The first was from the Louis W. and Maud Hill Family Foundation, which funded library purchases over a five-year period as well as faculty development.[113] The second was a substantial gift which became the Musser Endowment Fund and has enabled Carleton to bring 30 visiting professors to campus since its inception. In 1973, Washington and Lee received a three-year Mary Reynolds Babcock Foundation grant. In 1985, the Cowles Foundation awarded Grinnell a grant to start a Chinese studies program, and Whitman received a gift from Y.C. Wang, a Taiwanese businessman, to start a Chinese program.[114]

In the 1980s, the Asian studies initiative at private colleges benefited from two other developments. The first was the Immigration Act of 1965, which brought what one historian calls a "second wave" of Asian immigrants to this country.[115] Beginning in the 1980s, these immigrants and their children have been finding their way into American higher education, especially private colleges, creating there a new sort of Asian presence on campus. Colleges that once had only a few Asian and Asian American students now have contingents that compose anywhere from 3 or 4 percent to 20 percent of their student bodies. The growing numbers of students of Asian descent also has encouraged, no doubt, many administrators and faculty to create new positions in Asian and Asian American fields.

The spread of affirmative action programs is the other development that has affected the fortunes of Asian studies at private colleges. Just as the era of civil rights encouraged the hiring of women, affirmative action programs promoted the hiring of Asia specialists, many of whom are of Asian descent and thus can be counted as minorities. Thus, Asia specialists of Asian descent are doubly valuable to the institutions that hire them, a benefit that has had an unexpected impact on the composition of Asian studies programs at many private colleges.

It was in the 1960s, 1970s, and 1980s, then, that the formal study of Asia was firmly established at private colleges across the United States.

A number of developments made this possible. First was the availability of Asia specialists and their willingness to teach at the undergraduate level, as well as the commitment to Asian studies by administrators and faculty. In addition, the redefinition of general education in the late 1970s and the 1980s to include the non-Western world gave Asia a home in the undergraduate curriculum. Indeed, Asian studies may now be better integrated into the curriculum of private colleges and affecting more students than was the case at the big universities. Moreover, the generous support of charitable foundations, the federal government, and private individuals facilitated, and in some cases enabled, the establishment of Asian studies at private colleges. Finally, new developments in American education also have encouraged the development of Asian studies—the growing numbers of Asian American students and the pressure to hire minority faculty.

Conclusion

No single narrative tells the full story of the development of Asian programs at private colleges, and no simple recipe guarantees success. Asian studies developed differently at each institution, producing both successes and failures. Clearly, the development of Asian programs at private colleges has been the product of larger forces—a spiritual vision, wars, ideological conflict, and powerful commercial interests. The proliferation of Asian studies programs in the 1980s is telling in this regard. Furthermore, the shape of Asian studies programs at private colleges has nearly always reflected the vision of highly placed administrators, particularly presidents and deans, and faculty. Here the quality of the vision and the successful collaboration of administrators and faculty have been crucial and explain many of the success stories. Conversely, a flawed vision and the absence of such collaboration are usually the main reasons for the failures. Retrained faculty played, and continue to play, an important part in the development of Asian studies at private colleges. Their courses were the first and, for a long time, the only courses on Asia and continued to fill out the newly created Asian studies majors even after specialists were hired. This is still true at many institutions. Finally, Asian studies would never have developed at most private colleges in this country without the generosity of external donors, especially the big foundations. Indeed, it is the continuing commitment of these foundations—notably, the Ford, Luce, Freeman, Japan, Chiang

Ching-kuo, and Mellon foundations—and private donors that make the future of Asian studies at private colleges so promising.

Notes

The author wishes to thank Anjali Kamat and Edward Cho, research assistants, and all those who responded to requests for information contributing to this chapter.

1. Frederick Rudolph, *The American College and University, 72; Clarence Shedd, Two Centuries of Student Christian Movements*, 56–58.

2. David Titus, "A Brief History of East Asian Studies at Wesleyan," 13–14.

3. Shedd, *Student Christian Movements*, 73, 62.

4. Rudolph, *American College and University*, 170–72, 160, 58–59.

5. Laurence Veysey, "Stability and Experiment in the American Undergraduate Curriculum," 1.

6. Rudolph, *American College and University*, 52–53.

7. Shedd, *Student Christian Movements*, 94–120, 267.

8. Ellsworth C. Carlson, Oberlin in Asia, 3.

9. Merrill E. Jarchow and Leal A. Headly, Carleton, the First Century, 396–97.

10. Carlson, *Oberlin in Asia*, 19–20; John Scholte Nollen, *Grinnell College*, 113.

11. Grinnell College Sesquicentennial Chinese Studies Committee, *Grinnell and China in the Twentieth Century*, 1–3.

12. Charlie Brown Hershey, *Colorado College 1874–1949*, 214; Carl Price, Wesleyan's First Century, 238.

13. Rudolph, *American College and University*, 356.

14. William H. McNeill, *The Pursuit of Power*, 233–34.

15. Edward P. Crapol and Howard Schonberger, "The Shift to Global Expansionism, 1865–1900," 186–202.

16. *Kodansha Encyclopedia of Japan*, vol. 5, 386.

17. Jarchow and Headly, *Carleton, the First Century*, 326.

18. Carlson, *Oberlin in Asia*, 20; Thomas Hamm, *Earlham College*, 172.

19. Price, *Wesleyan's First Century*, 235.

20. Edward Seidensticker, *Kafu the Scribbler*, 18–31.

21. Hershey, *Colorado College 1874–1949*, 228.

22. Ray Moore, personal communication, June 27, 1999.

23. Lucy Lilian Notestein, *Wooster of the Middle West*, vol. 2, 38–39.

24. E. Wilson Lyon, *The History of Pomona College 1887–1969*, 257.

25. Caroline Beatty, personal communication, May 22, 1999.

26. Robert McCaughey, *International Studies and Academic Enterprise*, 84.

27. Titus, "East Asian Studies at Wesleyan," 14.

28. McCaughey, *International Studies and Academic Enterprise*, 84–85.

29. Ann May, personal communication, July 1, 1999; Stanley Mickel, personal communication, July 6, 1999.

30. David Deal, personal communication, June 30, 1999.

31. Edwin O. Reischauer, *My Life Between Japan and America*, 36–37.

32. Robert Entenmann, personal communication, August 11, 1999; Ray Moore, personal communications, June 28 and 30, 1999.

33. Charles Hucker, *The Association for Asian Studies: An Interpretive History*, 5; Robert McCaughey, "International Studies and General Education," 354.

34. Titus, "East Asian Studies at Wesleyan," 14.

35. McCaughey, *International Studies and Academic Enterprise*, 82, 88.

36. See Leonard Gordon, *Doctoral Dissertations on China*; Frank J. Shulman, *Doctoral Dissertations on Japan and Korea 1969–1979*.

37. McCaughey, "International Studies and General Education," 348–54; Veysey, "Stability and Experiment in the American Undergraduate Curriculum," 5–12.

38. Raymond Fosdick, *The Story of the Rockefeller Foundation, 1913 to 1950*, 24–25, 86–91.

39. Hucker, *Association for Asian Studies*, 6.

40. John King Fairbank, *Chinabound*, 98, 115; Reischauer, *My Life Between Japan and America*, 42.

41. Caroline Beatty, personal communication, May 22, 1999; Lyon, *History of Pomona College 1887–1969*, 343. See also chapter three by Stanley Mickel.

42. Reischauer, *My Life Between Japan and America*, 41.

43. Fairbank, *Chinabound*, 100, 167.

44. Reischauer, *My Life Between Japan and America*, 85.

45. Fosdick, *The Story of the Rockefeller Foundation*, 249–50.

46. Ibid., 250.

47. Fairbank, *Chinabound*, 100; Fosdick, *The Story of the Rockefeller Foundation*, 198; John Lindbeck, *Understanding China*, 36.

48. Fairbank, *Chinabound*, 180; Lyon, *History of Pomona College 1887–1969*, 361; Reischauer, *My Life Between Japan and America*, 86.

49. David Gonzalez, "John K. Fairbank."

50. Reischauer, *My Life Between Japan and America*, 91–94, 96–97, 104–109.

51. Fairbank, *Chinabound*, 312, 315; Reischauer, *My Life Between Japan and America*, 109.

52. Fairbank, *Chinabound*, 396.

53. Ibid., 355.

54. Reischauer, *My Life Between Japan and America*, 161–304.

55. Hucker, *Association for Asian Studies*, 7; Hawaii Nikkei History Editorial Board, comp., *Japanese Eyes American Heart: Personal Reflections of Hawaii's World War II Nisei Soldiers*, 7; Pedro Loureiro, personal communication, July 30, 1999.

56. Gordon, *Doctoral Dissertations on China*, 158, 46, 70.

57. Shulman, *Japan and Korea*, 213.

58. Gordon, *Doctoral Dissertations on China*, 70; Shulman, *Japan and Korea*, 189–90.

59. Hawaii Nikkei History Editorial Board, *Japanese Eyes American Heart*, 423.

60. Wendell Bennett, *Area Studies in American Universities*, 15.

61. Dan Balik, personal communication, June 23, 1999; Registrar, Colgate University, personal communication, June 22, 1999.

62. Hyman Kublin, "Brooklyn College," 12–13, 17.

63. Ron Lithcome, personal communication, June 25, 1999; Hiroshi Miyaji, personal communication, August 9, 1999; Suzanne Barnett and Karl Fields, personal communication, June 25, 1999.

64. Lyon, *History of Pomona College 1887–1969*, 358.

65. *Pomona College Bulletin, Annual Catalogue 1940–41; Pomona College Bulletin, Annual Catalogue 1945–46.*

66. Carl Jacobson, personal communication, August 4, 1999.

67. Frank Lorenz, personal communication, June 24, 1999.

68. Titus, "East Asian Studies at Wesleyan," 14.

69. Hamm, *Earlham College*, 238, 245.

70. Ray Moore, personal communication, June 29, 1999.

71. Theodore Herman, "Colgate University," 20.

72. Hamm, *Earlham College*, 246.

73. Kublin, "Brooklyn College," 12.

74. Ibid., 13–14.

75. John Thompson, "Among Indiana Colleges," 33.

76. Ibid., 36–38.

77. Ibid., 39.

78. Ibid., 40.

79. Bennett, *Area Studies in American Universities*, 10–14, 17.

80. Richard Lambert, *Language and Area Studies Review*, 205.

81. Bennett, *Area Studies in American Universities*, 17.

82. Hucker, *Association for Asian Studies*, 103.

83. John W. Hall, "East, South and Southeast Asia," 162.

84. See Fairbank, *Chinabound*, 359.

85. William Nelson Fenton, *Area Studies in American Universities*, 82.

86. Ibid., 1.

87. Veysey, "Stability and Experiment in the American Undergraduate Curriculum," 57.

88. John W. Hall, "Beyond Area Studies," 51.

89. Veysey, "Stability and Experiment in the American Undergraduate Curriculum," 57.

90. Fenton, *Area Studies in American Universities*, 81–82; Lambert, *Language and Area Studies Review*, 3.

91. Hall, "Beyond Area Studies," 62, 52.

92. McCaughey, "International Studies and General Education," 365.

93. Fairbank, *Chinabound*, 355.

94. Lambert, *Language and Area Studies Review*, 2.

95. Hall, "Beyond Area Studies," 56–57.

96. McCaughey, "International Studies and General Education," 363–64; Jonathan Green, personal communication, June 18, 1999.

97. Fosdick, *The Story of the Rockefeller Foundation*, 251. Hall, "East, South and Southeast Asia," 161; Charles Hirschman, "The State of Southeast Asian Studies in American Universities," 50–51; Lindbeck, *Understanding China*, 77–85; Richard Magat, *The Ford Foundation at Work*, 43 (n. 21), 73, 104, 169, 179.

98. Lindbeck, *Understanding China*, 79.

99. Walter Guzzardi, *The Henry Luce Foundation*, 189–90.

100. Thomas Coburn, personal communication, June 30, 1999; Hiroshi Miyaji, personal communication, August 9, 1999; Robert Entenmann, personal communication, August 11, 1999.

101. McCaughey, "International Studies and General Education," 368–69.

102. Bardwell Smith, personal communication, June 28, 1999.

103. Bardwell Smith, "Asian Studies at Carleton."

104. Joan O'Mara, personal communication, August 11, 1999.

105. McCaughey, "International Studies and General Education," 371.

106. Suzanne Barnett and Karl Fields, personal communication, June 25, 1999; David Deal, personal communication, June 30, 1999; Joan O'Mara, personal communication, August 11, 1999.

107. Suzanne Barnett and Karl Fields, personal communication, June 25, 1999.

108. David Deal, personal communication, June 30, 1999.

109. Joan O'Mara, personal communication, August 11, 1999.

110. See chapter three by Stanley L. Mickel.

111. Titus, "East Asian Studies at Wesleyan," 15; Freeman Foundation, *1998 Annual Report.*

112. Thomas Coburn, personal communication, June 28, 1999; Ray Moore, personal communication, June 27, 1999; James Leavell, personal communication, May 14, 1999; Suzanne Barnett and Karl Fields, personal communication, June 25, 1999; Joan O'Mara, personal communication, August 11, 1999.

113. Bardwell Smith, "Asian Studies at Carleton," 278–79.

114. Bardwell Smith, personal communication, June 28, 1999; Joan O'Mara, personal communication, August 11, 1999; Leslie Czechowski, personal communication, June 8, 1999; David Deal, personal communication, June 30, 1999.

115. Ronald Takaki, *Strangers from a Different Shore*, 419–71.

3

Asian Language Study in Liberal Arts Colleges

Stanley L. Mickel

Asian language study is not only the foundation for an academic program that promotes an understanding of Asia; it is a key that opens another door to the liberal arts for students. In support of this statement, in this chapter I argue that not only is studying the language spoken in an Asian culture essential for understanding that culture and crucial to building an effective program in Asian studies, but also it stimulates the overall intellectual climate at a liberal arts school and expands the intellectual horizons of the faculty and students alike. This chapter outlines the development of the study of East, South, and Southeast Asian languages in the United States. Following this is a brief discussion of the evolution of the major schools of pedagogies used to teach foreign languages in the past century. The fourth section discusses the various ways a liberal arts college can organize an Asian language curriculum. Ending the chapter is a list of funding agencies that have provided support in the past for Asian studies programs.

The Value Asian Language Study Adds to a Liberal Arts Degree

Technology is making the world in which we live increasingly smaller and more immediate, but, conversely, heightened sensitivity to cultural diversity is making our world ever larger and more complex. At the same time, the cultural, economic, political, and military importance of Asia to America has grown dramatically over the last decades. In this incessantly changing world, a world in which problems increasingly cross national borders and require cooperative solutions, studying an Asian language and the culture to which it gives voice is valuable in many ways to both students and their colleges.

Academic institutions benefit when the study of Asian languages and cultures is part of the curriculum. Whether they are about history, religion, fine arts, political science, literature, or another discipline, courses with an Asian content introduce a universe of ideas that stimulate faculty and student interest in new and challenging directions. This happens because Asian studies courses not only provide informative comparisons with traditional Western European–based values; study of the similarities and differences between the many cultures of East, South, and Southeast Asia suggests much about the foundations of all human thought and behavior. An Asian studies curriculum also helps students prepare for the multicultural world in which they will live and work in the twenty-first century. A variety of professions—environmental protection, government, business, medicine, and law among others—will increasingly present students with situations in their jobs that reach across national boundaries. Students will need to know how to use their professional skills in cooperation with peoples from other countries whose actions are based on different values. In order to effectively do so in Asia, it is essential that they are proficient in Asian languages and cultures. Those institutions that offer training in Asian studies demonstrate their intellectual vitality and are more attractive to students who want to be at the forefront of their professions. In addition, Asian American students are matriculating in growing numbers at liberal arts colleges, and they look to these institutions to offer courses that provide knowledge about their ethnic heritages.

Students of an Asian language grow intellectually in the many ways all students of foreign languages do: they strengthen their ability to think analytically and critically, they gain the self-confidence and self-discipline that come with mastering a demanding body of knowledge, they gain flexibility and tolerance from dealing with new and difficult situations, they learn much about their own language when examining and comparing it with a different language, and they also gain many insights into the people and culture of the target language community. In addition, they learn a skill that will forever be important: how to communicate with someone in another language.

Asian language study also stimulates intellectual development in unique ways. For example, the grammatical structures of many Asian languages differ from those of European languages in ways that reveal new and provocative modes of thought: Chinese nouns and pronouns are free of gender markers. Does this suggest that Chinese society has fewer gender-related issues? Culturally valued clarity about relative social status is unavoidably conveyed in Japanese sentences by the verb endings employed. What does this say to Americans nurtured on egalitarian principles? The principal South Asian language, Hindi, has a highly detailed grammatical structure that shares ancestral features with European languages. What are American students to make of that? As students ponder linguistic features such as these, they gain a deeper understanding of Asian cultural values and, potentially, of themselves and their own culture.

Other illuminating bits of knowledge come unexpectedly through study of an Asian language; for example, the character writing system of East Asia contains many characters whose graphic shapes suggest the way the Chinese and those who use this writing system conceptualize the world. Consider the character for "middle" or "center" that is part of the name of the country "China." This usage both suggests the Chinese view of China's central place in the world and echoes the traditional Chinese concept that Chinese culture is at the heart of what it means to be civilized. The character for "female" is an evolution from the original graph that showed a figure sitting with hands passively crossed, an unforgettable message about the subordinate place of females in traditional Chinese culture. The Japanese writing system with its combined use of Chinese characters to convey concepts and a phonetic syllabary evolved from Chinese characters to mark phonetic values is eloquent evidence of the unique ability the Japanese have to adopt and adapt foreign concepts. That the Koreans invented their own syllabic writing system more than 550 years ago but continued to use Chinese characters until recently tells much about the cultural and political history of the Korean people. Simply knowing that writing systems based on Sanskrit are used throughout South Asia and some of Southeast Asia gives students an understanding of the historical flow of events in those regions. When students observe that contemporary Indonesians use a writing system based on the Western alphabet, they are unforgettably reminded of the colonialism and cultural imperialism that Indonesia endured over the past two centuries.

Additional benefits of Asian language study come when students are graduated and seek employment. They will find that proficient language abilities and cultural sensitivities that enable a student to function smoothly across cultures have become everyday features of both domestic and international careers. Whether exchanging simple greetings with a salesclerk or negotiating subtle details of an agreement with the head of a governmental bureau, a person who has studied an Asian language and its culture has a clear advantage over someone with equal professional skills who knows nothing about them. Evidence of proficiency in an Asian language is a powerful element in a bachelor's degree. Business is the application that usually comes to mind in thinking of potential career applications for those with knowledge of an Asian language, but resurgent cultural pride in all areas of Asia makes it mandatory that those who wish to effectively interact with Asians be able to use the local language in a wide variety of professional fields. Foreign Service personnel who want to function successfully in Asia and be truly in touch with the national mood need to be able to communicate with the citizens in their own language and to read their newspapers. Scientists who want to keep up with developments in Asian science are advised to be able to read scientific abstracts written in an Asian language. Journalists, who depend for their livelihood on being able to dig out information, will find the digging much more productive, and more verifiable, if they can ask questions in the local language. Missionaries who want to be successful have a head start if they are prepared to carry out their duties using the language spoken in their community. Furthermore, while communication on the Internet is predominantly conducted in English at present, national pride is leading to more use of local languages in electronic communication.

Within the United States as well there is a range of situations that require a knowledge of Asian languages; for example, government agencies from the State Department to the Customs Service seek employees proficient in Asian languages and cultures, the travel industry benefits when its workers can communicate effectively with its Asian customers, and professional translators are sought after for conferences and publications. These and the many other needs that exist underscore the probability that the demand for teachers of Asian languages will grow in the decades ahead.

An interest in Asian studies has been a feature of American academic life for more than a century, although until the recent past this interest had been confined to a tight circle of elite graduate institutions. The following section will provide an outline of the evolution of the study of East

Asian, South Asian, and Southeast Asian languages in the United States during the past 100 years.

Historical Background of Asian Language Study in America

The first efforts to teach Asian languages in the United States came in the late nineteenth century.[1] In the time since then, interrelated geographical, political, and economic factors have deeply influenced the specific languages studied and the growth of Asian language study in America. The impact of geography can be seen in the fact that China, Japan, and Korea each have one official language, which allows students to efficiently concentrate their educational efforts. This is not the case in most of Southeast and South Asia; for example, India has seventeen languages given official national or regional status in its constitution. The start of World War II initiated a period wherein world events increased interest in teaching and learning Asian languages, mostly Japanese and Chinese, in the United States. The interest in Asian affairs was further stimulated by subsequent political events as momentous as the Cold War and the wars in Korea and Vietnam. In addition, over the past several decades, economic developments as profound as Japan's economic miracle, China's policy of opening up to Western investment in the 1980s, and recent fluctuations in the financial health of Asian countries have stimulated or depressed interest in learning about Asia and its languages. The interaction of these factors with events in America as disparate as McCarthyism in the early 1950s, "Ping Pong diplomacy" in the 1970s, and the growth of a culturally diverse society in the 1990s has led to an uneven development of the study of Asian languages in America over the past century.

Yale University is credited with starting, in 1877, the first Chinese language and literature lectureship in the United States.[2] The next school to teach Chinese was the University of California at Berkeley, which established a department of Asian languages in 1896. However, before World War II, it was generally only because of the academic interests of individual scholars at a half-dozen or so research institutions such as Columbia University, the University of Chicago, and Harvard University that studying the Chinese language was possible.[3] Pomona College, which offered a course in elementary Japanese and started offering Chinese language courses in 1939, is an exceedingly rare example of a private liberal arts school that offered Asian languages in this earlier period. World War II and the establishment of the People's Republic of China in 1949 resulted in many Chinese scholars coming to America, and in a heightened awareness of the strategic importance of Chinese language study. Instruction in the language grew slowly but fairly steadily as some of these scholars expanded on the prewar base and established programs in Chinese language and literature, mainly at research centers such as Stanford University, Indiana University, and the University of Hawaii.

The onset of the Cold War in the late 1940s resulted in many hundreds of people learning Chinese at the Army Language School (later called the Defense Language Institute) in Monterey, California, and at the U.S. government's interagency School of Language Studies at the Foreign Service Institute in Washington, D.C. The Cold War also brought about educational programs sponsored by the federal government such as the National Defense Foreign Language (NDFL) fellowship program which, among other things, promoted the study of Asian languages at the graduate school level.[4] Many of the people trained under these programs continued on to become academic professionals in the field of Chinese language education. A few private liberal arts institutions, such as Oberlin College (1965), Wellesley College (1966), Wittenberg University (1970), and Middlebury College (1976, summer school in 1966), were leaders in this period of growth in Chinese language instruction at undergraduate colleges, but it was not until Deng Xiaoping's political and economic opening up of China in the 1980s that a larger number of liberal arts schools established Chinese language programs. Williams College (1984), Beloit College (1985) and Augustana College (1988), among many other schools, started Chinese instruction during this period. Initially, instructors for these programs often came from the ranks of Americans trained at U.S. government language schools for military and diplomatic duties; subsequently, the events of June 1989 in Tiananmen Square led more Chinese intellectuals to come to America and teach the Chinese language.

Charitable foundations have also had an influential role in developing Chinese studies in America. Grants from the Chiang Ching-kuo Foundation have funded the establishment of more than 60 positions in Chinese language and literature at American institutions since 1989.[5] Also to be noted is the effort of the Dodge Foundation in the 1980s to encourage Chinese language study at the high school level. The growth in Chinese language enrollments from 1960 to 1995 can be seen in Table 3.1(page 59).

The first time the Japanese language was taught at the collegiate level in the United States was at the University of California at Berkeley in 1900. Another school or two on the West Coast began offering Japanese after that, but on the eve of World War II there were only 10 universities in all of the United States where Japanese could be studied, and it was generally taught at the elementary level only. Conflict between the United States and Japan in World War II brought about a radical change in this situation. The U.S. Navy and Army both opened schools that over the course of the war trained nearly 10,000 personnel to various degrees of proficiency in the Japanese language. While the vast majority of these people forgot about their language training after the war ended, there was a core of around 250 people who went on to academic careers focused on Japan.

Although the fellowships that the NDFL program later provided were primarily given to students of languages spoken by citizens of Cold War adversaries such as China and Russia, some scholarships were given to support the study of the language of our ally, Japan. This had the effect of stimulating interest in Japanese as well, and there was a gradual growth in the number of Americans studying the Japanese language and culture through the mid-1970s.[6]

Interest in Japanese language instruction at liberal arts colleges had its greatest surge of growth in response to the astounding success of the Japanese economy in the 1970s and 1980s. Programs were established at Wittenberg University (1971), Earlham College (1975), Williams College (1985), Skidmore College (1989), and many other schools during this period. Japan's economic success led to greater numbers of American undergraduates having a vision of learning Japanese as part of a professional career dealing with Japan. The National Association of Self-Instructional Language Programs (NASILP) provided initial leadership in meeting the need for Japanese language instruction. Even more significantly, in 1974 the Japan Foundation started a grant program designed to place study of the Japanese language in the mainstream of foreign language study in the United States. From 1974 to the present, the Japan Foundation has funded more than eighty Japanese language faculty positions at American colleges and universities.[7] (The Japan Foundation has also funded many language positions at the secondary school level.) As can be seen from Table 3.1, in the fall of 1995 Japanese was the Asian language with the highest number of students enrolled in the United States.

Table 3.1

Registrations in the Ten Leading Modern Foreign Languages in Selected Years with Percentage Change (abridged)*

Language	1960	1970	1980	1990	1995
Arabic	541	1,333	3,446	3,475	4,444
		+146.4%	+160.0%	+0.3%	+27.9%
Chinese	1,844	6,238	11,366	19,490	26,471
		+238.3%	+82.2%	+71.5%	+35.8%
French	228,813	359,313	248,361	272,472	205,351
		+57.0%	−30.9%	+9.7%	−24.6%
German	146,116	202,569	126,910	133,348	96,263
		+38.6%	−37.3%	+5.1%	−27.8%
Japanese	1,746	6,620	11,506	45,717	44,723
		+279.2%	+73.8%	+297.3%	−2.2%
Russian	30,570	36,189	23,987	44,626	24,729
		+18.4%	−33.7%	+86.0%	−44.6%
Spanish	178,689	389,150	379,379	533,944	606,286
		+117.8%	−2.5%	+40.7%	+13.5%
Total Registrations	1,127,363	924,837	1,003,234	1,184,100	1,138,772

*Richard Broad and Bettina J. Huber, "Foreign Language Enrollments in United States Institutions of Higher Education, Fall 1995," 4. Note that this table is for the fall semester only; it does not include summer schools or the remainder of the school year. Also note that it includes language students registered for courses at two-year colleges through graduate schools, not just liberal arts schools. Figures for Hebrew, Italian, and Portuguese are also given in the original table but are omitted here for the sake of brevity. The table is quoted with permisson from the Modern Languages Association.

This table also demonstrates that the growth of Chinese and Japanese language study has not been matched by the study of other Asian languages. For example, Korean language courses were offered at Yale University as early as 1945, at the University of Washington in 1946, and at several other graduate institutions a few years later, but it is still unusual to find Korean language courses offered outside major research institutions. While interest in Korean language study has seen some growth in the 1990s, an examination of the 63 schools found on the Korean language list at the Web site for the Center for Advanced Research on Language Acquisition (CARLA) at the University of Minnesota, *http://carla.acad.umn.edu/lctl/lctl.html*, shows that Korean language study is virtually nonexistent at liberal arts schools.[8]

The early history of the study of South Asian languages in America paralleled that of East Asian languages. Harvard University established its Department of Sanskrit and Indian Studies in 1890, offering courses in Pali, Sanskrit, and Tibetan, and the University of California at Berkeley had its Department of Near East Languages in 1905, teaching seven South Asian languages. Other research institutions established Indian studies programs later; for example, Johns Hopkins University taught Hindi in 1943 and Cornell University started its India Program in 1953.[9] The study of South Asian languages, however, did not experience the growth East Asian languages did after World War II, and there is very little formal instruction presently available for liberal arts students. There are notable exceptions such as Davidson College with its impressive range of South Asian courses and Carleton College, which teaches Marathi to support the study abroad program organized by the Associated Colleges of the Midwest; but most students who want to learn a language such as Tamil or Urdu have no choice but to take an independent study, if a cooperative professor is available, or go on a study program in South Asia.

Rarest of all to find is even one of the many languages of Southeast Asia offered at liberal arts schools. While there are 11 well-established and successful Southeast Asian language programs at graduate schools such as Cornell University, Ohio University, and Northern Illinois University, virtually the only way for a student at a small liberal arts institution to study a language such as Thai, Indonesian, or Burmese is to arrange for an independent study program with an interested faculty member, work privately with a fellow student from the country where the language is spoken, or pursue a self-study tape program (for example, NASILP) or tele-distance instruction using the Internet.[10] In the past decade, however, a number of students have moved ahead of their institution's formal curriculum and developed a Southeast Asian language capability by going on a Council on International Educational Exchange (CIEE) or School of International Training (SIT) study abroad program and then attending a summer program offered by the Southeast Asian Studies Summer Studies Institute (SEASSI), and/or going to a program in Thailand, Vietnam, or the Philippines for more advanced language study.[11] These students do not show up in formal enrollment figures, but they do suggest hope for further development in the study of the languages of Southeast Asia.

The CARLA Web site at the University of Minnesota (*http:// carla.acad.umn.edu/lctl/lctl.html*) provides a useful overview of the numbers of schools that teach Asian languages in the United States, although liberal arts schools are not listed as a separate category. There is great variation in the kinds of schools included, in the levels of offerings, and in the timeliness of the information, so the numbers given must be used with caution. Nonetheless, of note is that CARLA lists 599 institutions of higher education that offer instruction in Japanese, 331 schools that teach Chinese, and 63 that offer Korean. With the exception of Sanskrit (48 schools), Vietnamese (24 schools), Indonesian (24 schools), and Thai (21 schools), the other South and Southeast Asian languages are each taught at fewer than 5 schools in the United States.

To these totals may be added the self-instruction program organized by NASILP. Enrollment figures are not given, but a listing of the forty-some languages the association supports may be viewed at Web site *http://www.NASILP.org.*

Pedagogical Approaches to Foreign Language Instruction

The "grammar-translation" method of foreign language instruction held sway in the late nineteenth century and much of the first half of the twentieth century. It consisted of rote learning of grammatical rules and lists of vocabulary that were used to translate literary texts from the foreign language into the student's native language. Generally regarded as a form of mental exercise effective in developing intellectual muscles more than an actual effort to learn a foreign language, this method had as its pedagogical goal leading students to an understanding of outstanding examples of literature in the target language and simultaneously to a clearer understanding of their own language. One major disadvantage from the viewpoint of modern foreign language instruction was a nearly total lack of opportunities to speak or hear the target language.[12]

Increased opportunities to travel to foreign countries in the late 1800s led many people to have a greater need for an ability to speak foreign languages. The "direct method" was a pedagogical response to this new need. This method consists of learning a foreign language as a child would, by listening to it in large quantities and then associating it directly with objects and actions in everyday life without any use of the student's native language. Perhaps the most famous practitioner of this method was Joseph Berlitz. Some language pedagogues claimed that a significant drawback to this pedagogical approach is that, in the absence of structured introduction and grammatical explanations, students quickly internalized errors and found it difficult to understand or produce correct structures. This could lead to permanently lower competency levels and a concomitant inability to function at sophisticated levels. Other teachers did not see this problem. The "direct method" had some success, but nonetheless, "grammar translation" remained the predominant form of foreign language instruction until the advent of World War II.

The great need for people capable of speaking and understanding the languages of America's adversaries in World War II and at the beginning of the Cold War greatly advanced the use of the "audio-lingual approach." This aural/oral–based methodology combined principles of psychological behaviorism with the interest structural linguists have toward recurring patterns of oral speech. The result was a form of language study based on thoroughly mastering carefully selected patterns of speech in the target language. The goal is to imprint students with correct examples of the language in expectation that they could then use them as a secure base to function in the language in real life situations. Language labs filled with reel-to-reel tape recorders and students in headphones was one unforgettable feature of this approach. This pedagogy began to lose popularity when it became apparent that students tended to be unable to function in the target language beyond the particular patterns introduced in the classroom. The lack of attention given to reading and writing is also considered a clear disadvantage of this style of teaching. Audiolingualism dominated language teaching in America in the 1950s and 1960s, but in the 1970s it started to give way to various approaches based on cognitive theories of language learning.

Cognitive language learning pedagogies began their ascendency in the late 1950s with the development of Noam Chomsky's linguistic theories, which focus on the idea that all human languages have certain innate grammatical elements in common. By the late 1960s, scholars of second language acquisition were interpreting cognitive language learning to mean that students were to be guided toward developing control over the "universal grammar" elements present in the foreign language they were studying. Students were to build a competence that combines a priori control of the universal rules of language with an understanding of how languages generally function to enable them to engage in creative responses to real life situations involving the target language. An important feature of this pedagogy was that use of language is to be meaningful rather than the rote and lifeless recitation of sounds that often resulted from the audio-lingual approach.

A school of thought very influential in working toward the goals that developed from the theories of cognitive language learning was Stephen

Krashen's theory of the "monitor model." Briefly summarized, this theory involves students acquiring a second language by imitating the subconscious process children use to learn a first language. At the same time, students also consciously learn and apply the vocabulary and grammatical features found in the target language for use as a correcting "monitor" when communicating in the second language. Language is taught by presenting quantities of "comprehensible input" in a naturally ordered sequence in a relaxed classroom atmosphere that allows students to be receptive to learning. Other scholars have proposed relying more heavily on understanding the mental process involved in gaining and using knowledge, and then showing students how to apply those processes to foreign language learning. Other schools of cognitive language teaching are the "silent way," which uses a syllabus listing grammatical items and vocabulary to lead the student to learn through discovery and problem solving, while having minimal communication with the instructor; "suggestopedia," which uses relaxation techniques to make students psychologically receptive to foreign language materials; "community language learning," which calls for a teacher who serves as a passive resource person to aid groups of students who have the same learning goals; and "total physical response," which attempts to teach a foreign language through physical activity.

In the 1980s and 1990s there was a waning of enthusiasm for trying to find a perfect methodology for teaching foreign languages. Instead, the focus has been on creating classroom conditions that help students achieve "communicative competence." The end goal of communicative competence is to teach students to be proficient in using the target language to communicate with native speakers of the language. In this learner-centered pedagogy, instructors use an eclectic assortment of pedagogical strategies and tactics to guide students toward attaining specific degrees of proficiency in hearing, speaking, reading, and writing in the target language. Cultural understanding is also important.

A side result of the interest in proficiency has been a search for a way to state as objectively as possible the different levels of ability students may have with a foreign language. Building on earlier efforts by the Educational Testing Service and the U.S. government's Foreign Service Institute, the American Council on the Teaching of Foreign Languages (ACTFL) developed a scale in 1982 that articulates different levels of proficiency in speaking, listening, reading, and writing a foreign language. It divides proficiency with language skills into four basic levels, the first three of which have sublevels: novice (low, mid, high), inter-mediate (low, mid, high), advanced (advanced, advanced plus), and su-perior. Space does not allow listing all the details of each level and sublevel here, but a sample of the criteria set for the intermediate level will give a sense of the overall structure of the guidelines. Intermediate-level skills are given because this is the level that the majority of majors and minors in Asian languages reach during their collegiate career. (Note that while cultural skills are not separately articulated they are recognized as functional aspects of proficiency.)

Speaking: Low: Can ask and answer questions on very familiar topics, initiate and respond to simple statements and maintain very simple face-to-face conversations. Mid: Beginning to show some grammatical accuracy in basic constructions; vocabulary beginning to include personal history, leisure-time activities, etc. High: Beginning to show some spontaneity in language production; can initiate and sustain a general conversation; ability to describe and give precise information still limited.

Reading: Low: Can understand simple connected material in printed form; understands main ideas of simple announcements, forms of address, inquiries about family and friends. Mid: Can comprehend simple discourse for informative or social purposes, such as announcements of sports events, concerts, movies and some simple narration. High: Can comprehend a simple paragraph for information or recreational purposes; can identify main ideas from high-interest or familiar news publications and from descriptive material on daily life.

Listening: Low: Can understand utterances on basic survival needs, minimum courtesy expressions and travel requirements, and on very familiar topics can understand non-memorized material and face-to-face conversations. Mid: Can understand conversations on personal history, leisure-time activities, and short public announcements. High: Beginning to understand more extensive biographical information, home, office, school and shopping activities; cannot sustain understanding in unfamiliar situations.

Writing: Low: Can write short messages, such as simple questions and notes, postcards, etc. Mid: Able to compose short paragraphs, write about likes and dislikes, daily routine, autobiographical information, with the beginnings of grammatical accuracy. High: Can write simple letters, synopses and paraphrases, and short compositions on familiar topics.[13]

In addition to these proficiency guidelines, ACTFL has recently produced the Standards for Foreign Language Learning, which cover (1) communication (in languages other than English), (2) culture (knowledge and understanding of other cultures), (3) connections (with other disciplines), (4) comparisons (to develop insight into the nature of language and culture), and (5) communities (participate in multilingual communities at home and around the world). Specific standards are also being developed for 8 languages, two of which are Chinese and Japanese. Once completed, the specific standards for the eight languages will be combined with the generic standards into a single volume. See the ACTFL Web site *http://www.actfl.org/htdocs/standards/standards.htm* for an executive summary and e-mail addresses.

Building an Asian Language Curriculum at a Liberal Arts College

There are several intertwined questions to be faced when designing an Asian language curriculum: which language or languages to teach, what the student pool for each language is, what curricular structure the language offerings can take, what outcome goals best fit the students' intellectual and professional needs, what supporting curriculum the institution offers for an Asian studies program, what technological support the institution can give to foreign language study, and what sources of outside funding are available. These questions will be addressed separately below, but they all come together to form the structure of a foreign language program.

What Language or Languages Should Be Taught?

Because few liberal arts colleges have the resources to offer more than one Asian language, one answer to the question of what language or languages to teach lies in an analysis of the relative cultural, economic, and political importance of the Asian countries in the world. For example, over the past half-century, Japan and China, both possessors of a long and proud cultural heritage, have steadily grown in importance as players on the world stage. Their emergence has generated a range of career opportunities for students competent in their languages, which has attracted more students to the languages.[14]

Which languages will be taught also depends on who the prospective learners are and what their academic and career goals are. In addition to "true beginners" who want to learn an Asian language for the sheer pleasure of it and/or for use in a professional career, the past two or three decades have seen increasing numbers of Chinese American, Japanese American, and Korean American "heritage learners" interested in learning their ethnic language. There are also many children of immigrants from Asian countries such as India and Vietnam who want to learn about their parents' mother language. Whichever language or languages are chosen, it is common sense that the official language of the country rather than a regional dialect should be taught.

When deciding which language to offer, the fact that Chinese and Japanese are the most commonly taught Asian languages in the United States should be considered. There are relatively well-developed bodies of pedagogical materials available for both languages, and there are associations of Japanese and Chinese language teachers dedicated to raising the pedagogical level of instruction. At present, Korean and the languages of South and Southeast Asia are not as well supported.

Length of study is an important factor. The U.S. State Department's Foreign Service Institute has designated Chinese, Japanese, Korean (and Arabic) as category 4 languages. This means that it takes students the longest period of study to reach a proficiency level in them. Many South and Southeast Asian languages are placed at the next longest level of time required to reach proficiency. Because these languages require a longer period of study than European languages to reach the same degree of proficiency, fewer students enroll in them. Institutions should be prepared to support smaller enrollments until the program has established itself and can draw larger numbers of students.

What Is the Student Pool?

The student pool for Asian language study at undergraduate liberal arts institutions may be divided into three groups, which of course often overlap. The first group is made up of students who are aware of the value that studying an Asian language brings to their intellectual growth and who want to learn an Asian language for the joy of knowing an entirely new way of communicating. The second group consists of students who want to learn an Asian language for value it adds to their set of professional skills. A non-Western cultures requirement in the curriculum can be a strong stimulus in the depth of these two pools of students. The third group of students are interested in Asian language for reasons of ethnic heritage.

The needs of this third group can bring complications to the structure of a language program. The situation for Chinese American "heritage learners" is a good example of this. Many speak a Cantonese dialect and have to learn the official Chinese language almost from scratch; others may speak the official language with ease but have significant pronunciation and grammatical problems; and yet others may speak very accurately but have learned little or nothing of the Chinese character writing system and are functionally illiterate. This phenomenon causes placement and programmatic problems for Chinese language instruction. Korean Americans and Japanese Americans do not have this linguistic complication, but the large number of official Indian languages fragments the pool of interested Indian American students and makes it difficult to decide which language to offer.

What Structure Can Language Instruction Take?

Contemporary language learning standards that call for achievement of communicative competency with proficiency at stipulated oral and written tasks drive the pedagogical shape of a language program. To guide students toward being able to use the target language to function within a foreign society, learning materials and classroom instruction should present models of linguistic forms and cultural behavior to be imitated. Literary creations should definitely be used in upper-level courses, but their aesthetic orientation and the idiosyncratic writing styles often found in fine literature argue that literature should not be a major factor in the curriculum of elementary and intermediate language courses. Because students have to be able to interact in culturally appropriate ways in the society that uses the language they are studying, the language program should be supported with as many courses in the history, political science, religion, and anthropology of the region as possible to help students gain cultural competency while they are gaining communicative competency.

With these expectations in mind, there are four structures possible for language programs: self-study, college course work in a nonintensive curriculum, intensive summer institutes, and study abroad. While discussed separately below, elements of all four formats can be intertwined to create a successful language program. The specific needs of institutions will inevitably vary, but the programmatic outline given below can be a blueprint useful in designing an Asian language program for undergraduate liberal arts institutions.

Self-Study Programs

The National Association of Self-Instructional Language Programs provides organizational oversight for a program of study that features students using technology such as tape recorders, software packages, and the Internet combined with drill work provided by a native speaker of the target language. These programs can be successful with highly motivated and disciplined students. Contact *http://www.NASILP.org* for further details.

Students may also work on an independent study basis with a faculty member from another academic discipline who is competent in the target language. Campus politics can make this instructional avenue problematic, and, because so much depends on the enthusiasm of an individual faculty and students rather than on support from the college, interest can quickly evaporate. Video conferencing also makes it possible for students to have visual contact with distant speakers and examiners in self-study courses.

College Courses

This category refers to Asian language courses that are provided as a regular part of a college curriculum. Ideally, an effective undergraduate Asian language curriculum will provide four years of instruction by a team composed of two or more full-time faculty members. At least one instructor will be a successful learner of the language who can provide a model of how to study the language; the other instructor (or instructors) will be a native speaker of the language who has experience and skill at teaching the language to English speakers. The first two or three years of instruction will focus on guiding students toward accomplishing specified degrees of proficiency in all five areas found in a well-structured foreign languages program: speaking, hearing, reading, writing, and culture. The last year or so of language study can then focus on areas of specific interest to the faculty and students. Literature written in the target language should be taught at the higher levels after students have gained control of the standard features of the language. (Courses featuring the literature in English translation are often effective recruiting devices for language courses.)

A shortcoming of this curricular format is that instruction is usually limited to an hour a day for three to five days a week. Student attention and energies are also needed for other academic courses, and vacations are not usually devoted to foreign language study. Study can thus be somewhat sporadic with a loss of effectiveness. Nonetheless, a well-conceived and well-implemented college-level Asian language curriculum can bring students to desired levels of proficiency. When such a course of study is combined with a summer study and/or a study abroad program (as described below), students can achieve functional levels of proficiency even in category 4 languages by the end of their years of undergraduate study.

Videoconferencing offers an alternative way for schools to afford to offer college-level instruction for languages with low enrollments. For example, one college might offer classroom instruction in intermediate Japanese and have students at a second school participate in the class via video cameras; the second school could offer beginning Thai and have students from the other school use video cameras to "sit in" on that class. If the colleges are not too far from each other, participants can come together and use the target language to interact at points during the semester.[15]

Summer Courses

In this context, summer courses are programs of intensive study of an Asian language conducted in an immersion environment. In this environment communicative competency is nurtured and any use of English during the course of study is prohibited. Immersion programs typically feature four or more hours of daily classroom study followed by hours of language lab and tutoring work. Students live in accommodations dedicated to housing only students of the language, and they eat in dining halls in which only the target language is heard. Students can incorporate a summer or two of intensive language study as part of their overall work with the language and thus progress more rapidly.

Middlebury College is recognized as the "grandparent" of Asian language summer programs. Still highly successful after thirty years of instruction, Middlebury offers nine weeks of summer instruction in Chinese, Japanese, Korean, and Arabic as well as European languages (see *http://www.middlebury.edu/~ls*). Another well-established and well-structured program is the East Asian Summer Languages Institute (EASLI) at Indiana University, which offers eight weeks of immersion in Chinese, Japanese, and Korean language study every summer (*see http://*

www.indiana.edu/~easli). Beloit College offers Chinese, Japanese, and European languages as part of its annual nine-week summer school program (see *http://www.beloit.edu/~cls*). Many institutions, such as Yale University and the University of California at Berkeley, offer nonimmersion summer study in Asian languages. These courses are also helpful to students wishing to strengthen their Asian language skills and can form a useful adjunct to an undergraduate curriculum.

In the past two decades, intensive summer study programs have been established in Asia as well, for example, those in China. Princeton in Beijing is an immersion program based at the Beijing Normal University that gives students nine weeks of intensive instruction in Chinese, June through August. Duke University has a program that combines a summer of study in Beijing with a fall semester in Nanjing. Many programs require some prior language study, but there are also programs such as the CIEE summer program at Fudan University in Shanghai that accept beginning students.[16]

One shortcoming of immersion programs is that the rapid pace of instruction makes it very difficult for most students to retain all the materials presented. However, when used as part of a university curriculum that offers instruction to returning students at a continuing level, summer immersion programs can be effective in raising proficiency levels.

Study Abroad (and Internships)

Study abroad in this context of course refers to a summer, semester, or year-long period of study in the country where the target language is spoken. Study abroad is an undeniably valuable part of an established Asian language curriculum, and it can be a highly important component of Asian language study at schools that do not formally offer Asian language courses.

An inspection of *Academic Year Abroad: 1998/99* confirms that study abroad programs come in all shapes and sizes.[17] Some accept only students who have no prior language study, a few offer courses at the highest level, but most provide a range of study from the introductory to the advanced levels. Some programs give courses in the history, religion, literature, and politics of the area; others only offer language instruction.

Internships in a foreign country can be difficult to arrange, but there are some programs such as the Beijing Internship Program offered by Boston University that offer a variety of prearranged internship opportunities. The academic content of internships can be hard to evaluate, but students feel a tremendous payoff in using the language they have studied to communicate in a job setting and to establish relationships that can be valuable after graduation. Internships can be very helpful in building enthusiasm for Asian language study.

Study in the target language environment not only enhances language skills, it immediately brings the student into unavoidable contact with the core of a culture and forces the student to grapple with the very essence of the differences and similarities between cultures. Carefully chosen study abroad programs and well-structured internships are highly beneficial to students.

The Role of Technology in Language Instruction

The movement toward an eclectic pedagogy for teaching foreign languages has been greatly supported by a revolution in communication technology beginning in the last part of the twentieth century. Continual technological developments have opened up many stimulating and effective approaches to language teaching in general, and to the teaching of Asian languages in particular. Supplementing "old technology" such as chalk and blackboard, radios, and cassette players, "new technology" in the form of computers and their software programs on CD-ROMs and floppy disks, along with other new technologies such as satellite dishes and their live international programming, digitized video disks (DVDs), videoconferencing, laser disks, and the Internet with its ever-proliferating Web sites make opportunities for realistic language study constantly available and increasingly effective. When employed under the guidance of a pedagogical professional, modern technology is a powerful educational tool.

Availability differs by language, but currently there are software programs that show students how to write Asian scripts, packages that make vocabulary practice fun, interactive grammar drills, programs that spectrographically compare a student's pronunciation with that of a native speaker, interactive video packages, and many other programs. Web sites make it possible to travel to spots in Asia with the click of the mouse. Students can visit museums, sit in on meetings, inspect the menus of famous restaurants, and engage in many other activities that provide instant reinforcement of language skills and cultural understanding. The enhanced opportunities for linguistic and cultural interactions that technology provides in these and other ways make it possible for language learners to use the target language to handle a range of tasks in a lifelike environment that in the past they would have had to travel to a foreign country to experience. The continual, realistic language use that modern teaching structures provide can dramatically increase the appeal and effectiveness of foreign language study. A modern foreign language study program needs to have an up-to-date multimedia language lab.

It must be kept in mind, however, that while technology is an effective element of a well-structured program, it is not a magic mouse that brings Asian language competency with a single click. Computers cannot replace instructors, but they can infuse instruction with realia and stimulate students to aspire to function smoothly and with cultural sensitivity in the target language.

Summary

It is certain that language study is at the heart of Asian studies and that students can learn much about Asia and about themselves from it, but it should be kept in mind that a thorough understanding of any part of Asia demands much more. In addition to rigorous language study, an Asian studies program should be structured to lead students to investigate the history and political structures of the region. Students must also be familiar with the literatures and arts of Asia, and they definitely need to be conversant with the religious and philosophical traditions that motivate Asians. To learn an Asian language without knowing these and other aspects of the culture it gives voice to is to possess an empty vessel that is of misleading value.

Funding Organizations Historically Supportive of Elements of Asian Studies

The Andrew W. Mellon Foundation
140 East 62nd Street
New York, NY 10021

Chiang Ching-kuo Foundation for International Educational Exchange (USA)
8361 B Greensboro Drive
McLean, VA 22102

The Ford Foundation
Education and Culture Program
320 East 43rd St.
New York, NY 10017

The Freeman Foundation
Mr. Houghton Freeman
1880 Mountain Road, #14
Stowe, VT 05672

Fund for the Improvement of Postsecondary Education (FIPSE)
ROB-3, Room 3100
7th and D Streets, SW
Washington, DC 20202–5175

The Henry Luce Foundation
111 West 50th Street
New York, NY 10020

The Japan Foundation & Language Center in Los Angeles
2425 Olympic Boulevard, Suite 650E
Santa Monica, CA 90404–4034

The Korea Foundation
C.P.O. Box 2147
520 Namdaemunno 5–ga
Chung-gu, Seoul 100–095, Korea

The Pew Charitable Trusts
2005 Market Street, Suite 1700
Philadelphia, PA 19103–7077

The Starr Foundation
70 Pine Street
New York, NY 10270

Undergraduate International Studies in Foreign Language Program
U.S. Department of Education, Office of Post Secondary Education
Center for International Education
Washington, DC 20202–5332

The United Board for Christian Higher Education in Asia
475 Riverside Drive, Suite 221
New York, NY 10015

William & Flora Hewlett Foundation (tends to favor liberal arts institutions in California, Oregon, and Washington)
525 Middlefield Road, Suite 200
Menlo Park, CA 94025

Notes

1. The historical outline given in this chapter is not intended to be exhaustive but rather to identify pioneers in the field and to sketch the overall evolution of Asian language study in the United States.

2. Joseph Nathan Kane, *Famous First Facts*, 165. None of the other languages considered in this chapter are mentioned in this source.

3. Robert Hartwell, "The Study of Literary Chinese."

4. Part of the National Defense Education Act passed in August 1958, NDFL (National Defense Foreign Language), now called FLAS (Foreign Language and Area Studies), is a federally funded program that supports foreign language training at the graduate school level.

5. The Chiang Ching-kuo Foundation office verbally provided the number of schools and the dates for Chiang Ching-kuo grants in October 1998. There are no publications available that provide further information.

6. Akira Miura, "Japanese Language Teaching in the U.S.A." Most of the history of Japanese language study in America through the 1960s outlined here came from this source.

7. These numbers were most graciously provided by Eric Chow and Maki Uchiyama of the Japan Foundation. Records for 1974 and 1975 do not differentiate between the different types of positions funded, but in addition to the 71 language positions that were funded in 1976–1998, there were 13 grants given in 1974–1975.

8. Richard Broad and Bettina J. Huber, "Foreign Language Enrollments in United States Institutions of Higher Education, Fall 1995," 7. This page says that 3,343 students took Korean language courses in the United States in 1995.

9. Ward Morehouse, ed. *American Institutions and Organizations Interested in Asia*, 87–92, 109–11, 212–13.

10. Charles Hirschman, "The State of Southeast Asian Studies in American Universities." This study of the overall state of Southeast Asian studies in America focuses mainly on graduate school conditions, but undergraduate instruction is also considered.

11. I thank Roget Paget of Lewis and Clark College for pointing this out in a personal communciation of May 26, 1999.

12. The evolution of foreign language education in America in this century has been complex, especially since World War II, and only the most salient features are mentioned here. For more details see Alice Omaggio Hadley, *Teaching Language in*

Context, chapters 2 and 3. A handy reference for a brief historical overview and detailed comments on specific research topics in second language acquisition is William C. Ritchie and Tej K. Bhatia, ed., *Handbook of Second Language Acquisition*.

13. *ACTFL Proficiency Guidelines*.

14. See Christine U. Grosse, Walter V. Tuman, and Mary A. Critz, "The Economic Utility of Foreign Language Study," for a study of factors that influenced a group of MBA students in their decision of which foreign language to study.

15. In a personal communication of May 21, 1999, Rita Kipp reported that Kenyon College and Denison University have a Mellon Foundation grant to fund videoconferencing instruction in beginning Japanese and advanced Chinese.

16. Sara J. Steen, ed., *Academic Year Abroad: 1998/99*. Pp. 77–91 list 58 programs in China; pp. 91–95 list 15 for India; p. 95 lists two programs in Indonesia; pp. 95–113 list 86 programs in Japan; pp. 113–16 list 14 Korean programs; pp. 116–19 list 9 programs in Nepal; pp. 124–28 list 10 programs in Thailand; and a program or two are listed for Malaysia, for Singapore, for Taiwan, and for other locations.

17. Ibid.

4

Study Abroad in Asia

Stephen P. Nussbaum

Within the American classroom—or classrooms anywhere for that matter—the study of other cultures is always an unavoidably "heady" thing. Complex processes are reduced to paper and are discussed by students who rarely have intimate knowledge of the daily rhythms of life in the places being discussed. This process encourages misrepresentations of the dynamic ebb and flow of social life, and, indeed, these misrepresentations have acquired their own histories.[1] It seems essential that we seek opportunities to extend our classrooms to enable our students to engage firsthand the complexities of life elsewhere in the world. Study abroad in Asia enables students to encounter the diversities of Asia and brings them to know the daily rhythms of life in distant localities.

In thinking about this, one must recognize the character of the cultural immersion programs that remain the backbone of study abroad. By electing to incorporate a period of study in Asia within their college careers our students have chosen to take up a study of difference perhaps matched only by students of ancient civilizations. Unlike such students, however, they personally encounter age-old traditions springing from unfamiliar pasts and recently reshaped by colonial experiences, wars, ideologies, and the unrelenting changes brought to our social landscapes by modernity and its economic vagaries.

Study abroad, more than other academic experiences, presents participants with "total" educational experiences. It involves the full person and indeed springs from the play of embodied subjectivities. It challenges students to perform new roles in new languages. In doing this, it reveals dimensions of the human experience—the tacit assumptions of everyday life—in ways not accessible in single cultural settings. It takes students closer to the construction of sociality, of the shared but continually negotiated social norms that make life both intelligible and trying, than is possible by other methods.

Study abroad is a realm where generalizations about a people or their culture yield to ready affirmation as well as their own ultimate undoing in the observations and experiences of our students. We are poorly equipped to address life as it appears in the fleeting moments of its expression and even more poorly equipped to address how such life might be grasped by instruments, our students, who are full of hidden preferences regarding what they observe and how they process such observations. And we have few, if any, specialists to whom to turn.

As an emergent field within the American academy, the study of Asia in Asia is still in search of a critical vocabulary, preferred methods, and stable institutional homes.[2] In sketching the contours of this field, especially as it relates to liberal arts colleges, this chapter advances the following arguments: (1) Study abroad in Asia engages students in holistic learning processes similar to those found on the campuses of residential liberal arts colleges and is a logical extension of the learning styles, and in this sense the missions, of such institutions. (2) It catapults students to the forefronts of inquiry in several areas of the social sciences and humanities. (3) It epitomizes liberal inquiry and is integral to the educational activities of the liberal arts college of the twenty-first century.

These are not speculative arguments. They are based on the experiences of a significant number of liberal arts colleges and their students who have sought out study abroad experiences in Asia. A summary of the experience of American liberal arts colleges in Asia would require more space than is available here and must await another forum. In developing these arguments, where appropriate, I will rely on my experiences teaching at Earlham College and directing its undergraduate programs in Japan. Over 1,000 students from two midwestern consortia of liberal arts colleges have participated in these programs since their inception in the early 1960s. I will also argue that students traveling to most destinations in Asia share a set of substantive similarities springing from their encounter with noncognate languages and cultures that sets them apart from the vast majority of students participating in study abroad. This, rather than the vagaries of an imagined geography, is the defining character of study abroad in Asia.

In closing I will turn to the practical business of bringing students from American institutions to Asia and will outline some of the challenges those students and their home institutions face.

Study Abroad and the Colleges

At the outset it is important to distinguish between students participating in study abroad and international or foreign students. The latter category of students are seeking degrees from institutions outside their home countries. Often these are in relatively technical fields. Throughout the 1980s and 1990s the number of international students traveling from Asia to the United States increased dramatically. In the late 1990s there were about 500,000 foreign students in the United States, with more than half coming from Asia.[3] Japan is the second largest destination of Asian students with about 50,000 international students, mostly from China or Korea. Such students do not engage in study abroad as the term is used here.

Study abroad, conversely, is a field largely pioneered in the decades following World War II as part of an early wave of the globalization of higher education in the United States. It involves students traveling to destinations abroad to spend brief periods in intense study. This is often done in collaboration with local institutions and faculty who offer special courses for such students focusing on history, culture, and especially language education. In that participants on study abroad earn credit for graduation from their home institutions it is an integral part of the home campus curriculum.

Study abroad developed largely as a humanistic inquiry into the European heritage of contemporary America. In the United States there remains within the field a strong bias toward Europe. Two-thirds of the 100,000 participants in 1996–1997 sought destinations in Western Europe, and nearly one-quarter of these studied within the United Kingdom. These student flows both reflect geopolitical concerns linking the United States with Europe and reinforce class stratification within the United States.

Only 6 percent of the students from American institutions participating in study abroad in 1996–1997 traveled to Asia. Table 4.1 presents their destinations within Asia as well as the number of programs sponsoring their study.[4]

Only aggregate figures from all U.S. colleges are reported in Table 4.1. Considerable evidence suggests, however, that students from liberal arts colleges compose a significant portion of all students from American colleges studying in Asia. A recent study concluded that a greater percentage of students at the fifty most active "international" liberal arts colleges study foreign languages and participate in study

Table 4.1

Study Abroad in Asia: A Summary of Available Programs and Participants, 1996–1997

	Programs	Participants
Asia		6,046
Multisite	11	
Eastern Asia		4,477
China	59	1,627
Hong Kong		308
Japan	86	2,018
Korea, Republic of	15	380
Taiwan	5	144
South and Central Asia		781
Bangladesh		0
India	14	601
Kazahkstan		2
Kyrgyzstan		0
Nepal	10	151
Pakistan		0
Sri Lanka		26
Uzbekistan		1
Southeast Asia		788
Cambodia		1
Indonesia	4	209
Malaysia		43
Philippines		71
Singapore	1	180
Thailand	10	221
Vietnam	4	63
Asia, unspecified		0

abroad than in any other institutional category. Their closest competitors are the research universities. The graduates of such colleges regularly outnumber, on a per capita basis, the graduates of research universities in the production of Ph.D.'s in nearly all fields and in positions of leadership in international education, business, and government.[5]

The Residential Liberal Arts College and the Sociology of Education

While liberal arts colleges and the educational traditions they embody are well known in the United States, they are little known to readers from Asia. In this sense it is best to review characteristics of liberal arts colleges and, as possible, to outline the educational practices that set them apart from other institutions of higher education in the United States. It is important to note that such practices are not the exclusive preserve of the liberal arts colleges. Rather, because of their more intimate scale these colleges are where such characteristics can be seen with greater clarity and are likely to occur more regularly. The illumination of the characteristics and practices of liberal arts colleges is guided by the recent publication of *Distinctively American: The Residential Liberal Arts College* as a special issue of *Daedalus*.[6]

Throughout much of the twentieth century in the United States, a debate raged among educators—a debate concerning the relevancy of liberal learning. Are we better off focusing on distant classics to bring the world of our students—their past, present, and future experiences— under the gaze of the best thinkers, or are we better off focusing on nearby problems and, by teaching students to grapple with them, letting our students acquire the lifelong learning tools they most need? In the first part of the century one side of the debate was championed by John Dewey and his Progressive movement. Proponents advocated relevant education rooted in the world surrounding students. The other side was championed by Robert Maynard Hutchins, president of the University of Chicago, who advocated a classics-oriented educational experience.[7] Since the 1960s and 1970s a similar debate has taken hold, focusing on the canon and voices excluded from it.

It appears there has been general agreement, however, that liberal education involves introducing students to the experience of reading good books and to reflection on that experience. From reflection is born a liberating distance through which the student gains a new perspective on the human world. The vehicle for creating this distance has been an introduction to the great conversations, however they might be conceived, in the sciences, the humanities, and the social sciences. This is the goal of liberal education, as opposed to technical or practical education. It hinges on the ability of educators to relocate a student's understanding of the world. The recentering of students fosters their moral and intellectual development, nurturing the growth of the skills they will need to live in a complex and ever-changing social world. The roots of this style of education are quite old.[8]

While such liberal education has remained an important goal of American education, the demographics of higher education within the United

States have changed dramatically over the course of the last century and especially in the past 50 years. The number of people going to college increased from just over 2 million in 1950 to 14 million today. During the same period the number of students seeking graduate and continuing education expanded rapidly. Much of this growth was based on the use of public funds funneled to growing state universities. The proportion of students attending liberal arts colleges during this period has dropped from 25 percent of all students to about 2 percent.[9]

In a recent national study Alexander Astin has compared the effects of different types of educational institutions on their students. He argues that residential liberal arts colleges "produce a pattern of consistently positive student outcomes not found in any other type of American higher-education institutions."[10] He attributes this to the educational environments found at these institutions and particularly to their ability to foster student involvement. This is linked to the scale of these colleges, their residential character, and their strong student orientation. All these factors suggest that students learn best when they are involved with communities of learners. This involvement extends well beyond the classroom to the residence halls and the cocurricular life of the institution. He singles out the following five issues as particularly pertinent:

- small size,
- a residential program,
- a strong faculty commitment to student development,
- trust between students and administrators,
- generous expenditures on student services.[11]

The parallel between the student's involvement in the multiplicities of community life and a similar involvement with open-ended pedagogies of discussion, reading, and writing is notable. In both cases open-ended engagement is focused in a limited field, be it a residential community or a text. Students are encouraged to seek their own pathways in developing friendships and engaging in cocurricular activities, as well as in exploring academic interests. This self-directedness is often seen as the most important skill for students to develop.

Astin suggests that the holism of this view of learning has been lost in much of the rapid postwar expansion of higher education in the United States. Learning has come to be defined in terms of intellectual tasks, and efficiencies have been sought in the training of students in these tasks. University communities have come to resemble cities where involvement is always elective and fragmented. The result of these trends has been—from the perspective of the residential liberal arts college—the growth of impersonal, mass education.

In a widely read essay, Jean-François Lyotard has argued that a similar routinization of knowledge lies at the basis of the modern university. He suggests that the intellectual substance of education is dominated by universal themes, grand narratives, that are equally applicable to all times and places.[12] This is one of the legacies of the Enlightenment and its emphasis on the universalizing principles of science, on the one hand, and of democracy, on the other. There is no reason to suspect that knowledge as presented at liberal arts colleges has not also been powerfully shaped by these forces.

The rapid growth and dissemination of study abroad and international education particularly at such institutions, however, requires comment. Their lack of technical fields of study, combined with a traditional focus on particularism within the humanities and social sciences, appears to have created an environment where the exploration of other cultures came to be encouraged, especially during the 1960s and 1970s. The relatively intimate social contexts of these institutions and relatively streamlined decision-making processes played an equally important role in encouraging individual faculty members and small groups of students to begin experimenting in the study of other cultures. While modernization theory powerfully structured the curricula, there can be no doubt but that the search for other narrative conventions within distant cultures also became a pressing concern for many faculty and students. It is not accidental that Lyotard's work in the 1980s was foreshadowed by the work of multiple faculty at liberal arts colleges in the 1960s and 1970s.

Their work resulted in the birth of a new field, international education, with study abroad as one of its core components.[13] International education points to a field distinct from specialized programs in international studies or area studies. It has largely been developed on the campuses of residential liberal arts colleges in the United States and represents a reworking of an institution's curricula to acknowledge the global arena within which we are educating students. Only colleges such as Kalamazoo, Earlham, and Bowdoin can boast that the majority of their students can converse in a second language and have spent extended periods living and studying abroad. Only such colleges have grappled with what it means to incorporate the personal study of other languages and traditions into the education of all of their students.

The implication is that education is dependent on the social context of learning and that educational developments often spring as much from this context as from the intellectual issues of the day. If this is true then we must focus our attention on the contexts of learning our students encounter in Asia.

The Density of Everyday Life: Learning to Perform Within Noncognate Landscapes

Throughout the twentieth century and beyond there has been a growing recognition that we live in densely structured symbolic worlds. We grasp the world around us, we understand it, through representations often in the form of signs and symbols. Some of these refer to physical things in the world. Many refer to objects that exist only in thought. They are the stuff of our imagination. We are animals suspended within them, within webs of signification of our own making. Because of this, Clifford Geertz argues that our study of other peoples must be a hermeneutic one.[14] We are called upon to create interpretations of their lives and the institutions that shape them. More accurately, we need to develop interpretations of their own often diverse interpretations of their world. This process results in "thick" descriptions which are always incomplete. The density of other people's lives and the multiple understandings they share and contest with each other compose a tremendously dense landscape for interpretation.

Increasingly, arguments have mounted that we do not simply understand our world through signs. Rather, our use of signs as public codes is mediated by our situated embodiment. From our embodiment and daily routines emerge dispositions that shape us often in ways that are not fully conscious. Pierre Bourdieu, for example, argues that these dispositions create a habitus and that understanding this sphere of embodied activity is of crucial importance to the development of our study of human diversity.[15] Hans Joas, influenced in part by Dewey's pragmatism, recently has argued that to understand the creativity of human action we need to replace traditional models of rational choice with approaches that are based on a much more densely embodied reading of human activity.[16]

Joas cites Dewey, for example, as arguing that we are not intentional creatures so much as contextual creatures—our creativity springs from our close reading of contexts and the continual shifting of our own behavior to adjust to the changing landscapes we encounter and, through our actions, create. This means we are continually adjusting to the effects of our own actions as well as those of others. In doing this we are not seeing a world at a distance from ourselves and choosing to act in rationally optimum ways. Rather, before we even begin an action we are already anticipating certain reactions from the world. This anticipation shapes our actions and begins a series of feedback loops that continually frame the action as it unfolds. In focusing on embodied logics and situated action this approach is quite similar to Bourdieu's. This is part of a shift from thinking of culture as a code or sense of the "ought to be" existing at a distance from an actor to thinking of social action as unfolding and at best only partly shaped by general "rules." Intent and reflection are highly embedded in specific situations and often are powerfully shaped by dispositions that at the moment of action cannot be easily summarized and, indeed, are not the product of conscious reflection.

As we move toward situated approaches to understanding human behavior the centrality of language requires comment. Jerome Bruner, for example, has argued that it is language that permits "the construction and elaboration of that 'network of expectations' that is the matrix on which culture is constructed."[17] If this is true, then the density of everyday life is compounded for American students studying in Asia by the density of most Asian languages.

One of the most dramatic indicators of this comes from the Foreign Service Institute, the organization training American diplomats to speak the major world languages. These languages have been grouped into four categories indicating the amount of time required to train diplomats to usable levels of proficiency in each. All the major Western European languages fall into category 1. Languages like Hindi, Indonesian, and Malay fall into category 2, with category 3 including languages such as Thai, Vietnamese, Bengali, and Philipino.

In each case a student's proficiency is ranked on a scale of 1 to 4. Regarding category 3, John Hartman has commented as follows:

> For a superior "aptitude" FSI student . . . to achieve a 1/1+ rating (which correlates with "survival" language skills only), it would take 480 hours of instruction in the spoken language. Consider the fact that an intensive two-semester, 10–credit hour university course is only 340 classroom hours. Then the task of achieving spoken proficiency in a tonal Southeast Asian language, such as Thai, involves a great investment in time. . . . If anything, [this scale] helps to dramatize the long-term, lifetime dedica-

tion needed to achieve a high level of proficiency in Thai. . . . Because Thai is both a tonal language and one that employs an Indic-derived alphabet that attempts to preserve etymological spellings, it surely ranks as one of the more time-consuming languages, one that requires thousands of hours of exposure and practice. There is no such thing as a "short route" to learning Thai.[18]

Category 4 languages, Arabic, Chinese, Japanese, and Korean, are even more demanding. Three of four students in Asia from American institutions will study the languages in this last group. Viewed from the perspective of the native English-speaking student beginning his or her studies of another culture, this is a rough but telling measure of the density of the challenges awaiting the American student in Asia.

While learning a language includes learning syntax and vocabulary, these are not of its essence. They are merely steps in learning to move within the dispositions of the other person. The ultimate goal is to learn enough of those dispositions, and the linguistic and other structures shaping them, for the other person to realize that you are at home in his or her world—that you share with him or her a world that he or she finds familiar and comfortable.

This is a considerable challenge drawing on all of the embodied skills a student can develop. While the densities of the everyday worlds of Asia are substantial, considerable evidence suggests that students who study in Asia, far from finding these densities unfathomable, are absorbed by them.

Study Abroad: Compelling Liberal Inquiry

If engagement and reflection lie at the heart of liberal inquiry, and if this is best carried out in socially dense environments, then it is likely that study in Asia presents the densest learning environments available to an American undergraduate. Study abroad in Asia not only builds on the tradition of liberal inquiry, it is its culmination.

From the density of everyday life in Asia spring three characteristics of study abroad for American students: it is compelling, it provides an apprenticeship in cultural learning, and finally, it is part of a long-term engagement.

In rooting our students in the processes and rhythms of everyday life, well-crafted study abroad experiences engage their natural curiosity. In Eva T.H. Brann's terms they present students with matters that "compel" them. The daily life of the people surrounding them engages students; they need to comprehend it; they need to learn tb perform within it; and as their imagination expands they want to understand how it is structured by social and economic forces as well as those of tradition itself. Brann goes on to state that such "compulsion is the initial experience of truth."[19] For those students who are ready for this challenge, there is not likely to be anything within the curriculum of the liberal arts college that is as compelling as study in Asia. Certainly students who have studied in Asia understand this.

Well-structured programs turn the necessary vulnerability and engagement of students in understanding their immediate contexts into learning opportunities. They provide students, again in Brann's terms, with an encounter with wisdom. She states, "[The] 'human wisdom' spoken of in Plato's *Apology* is to know that one knows nothing, and to know it in two ways: as a highly specifiable lack and as an irrepressible longing."[20]

Study abroad is most effective when students can share their experiences and learn from each other. During study abroad, students become members of special transient interpretive communities. They typically share a common ignorance of the local community, its traditions, and its languages. Because of this, it not only demands their attention, it engulfs them. They are forced either to withdraw into expatriate worlds (an all too common reality) or to begin to engage in a close reading of their immediate environments. These become texts and, by collectively reading and responding to them, students learn more quickly. They encounter this new world from a unique starting point, one they share fully only with each other, and they move through several common phases in the development of their expanding understandings as they become comfortable with it. In gaining access to their daily necessities within that world, students build bridges between their prior worlds and the new one. In doing this they form an interpretive community based in locality yet linking distant texts (their prior worlds) to nearby concerns. Given the diversity of their collective backgrounds and interests and the interpersonally and textually rich environments within which they find themselves, study abroad comes to be characterized by relatively untargeted, tangible learning on the part of both individuals and groups of students.

This quality of tangible learning responds effectively to the challenges that Eugene M. Lang has argued face the liberal arts college. He argues that the traditional grounding of thought in issues beyond the academy needs to be revitalized. Drawing upon John Dewey, he presents an agenda for action, arguing that liberal arts education should (1) "engage students in the surrounding community," (2) focus on "problems to be solved rather than academic disciplines," and (3) "collaboratively involve students and faculty."[21]

In providing students with an apprenticeship in cross-cultural learning, study abroad fulfills Lang's requirements eloquently. It responds to the whole student and his or her life situation as well as those of people around them. It takes traditional academic discourses and ideally makes them speak to the condition of the student and field site. Economics, political science, and literature all become part of an interpretive grid students engage dialogically through the lens of personal experience. Able instructors aid students in doing this and assist them in learning to solve both the practical and the epistemological problems of their daily lives. They also teach students to train their imaginations to reach beyond their immediate environment to understand "distant" issues of import to faculty and their academic disciplines. Finally, by providing a rich human environment, study abroad encourages students to learn collaboratively from faculty and other local people.

Within this context the special roles of two local people are worth mentioning. The first is the language teacher and the second is the student's "key informant," often a host mother, a roommate, or a local college student. They provide students doing study abroad with many of their most valuable learning experiences, with an apprenticeship as much based on observation as on learning technical information about verbs, topics for conversation, or what clothes to wear to a party.

Among faculty members language teachers typically spend more time with students and see them more regularly than do other faculty. They get to know the full student and, perhaps more important, often have the full attention of the student. As everything in the experience of the student becomes a learning opportunity, a text to be transacted, the language instructor typically holds more clues to that text than anyone else a student encounters. Language instructors, because of their craft, often become the default guides to the local world. When they are successful at blending their concern with syntax and lexicon with their students' concern for establishing competencies in their daily lives, students unavoidably acquire great admiration, respect, and need of them.

Host mothers on programs featuring them are often of equal or even greater value. A host mother typically is available to the student at several points each day. She is concerned with the student's well-being and is likely to find herself accompanying the student to doctors, worrying about the hosted child's friends, or becoming upset with the student when he or she repeatedly seems not to be aware of something that either the host mother has explained or at least hinted at broadly. More than other local people, she "grounds" the student by sharing either directly or indirectly her expectations regarding everyday life. This includes conversations not only about the day's news in the neighborhood or the nation but also such things as how meals should be prepared and clothes washed. It extends to how one should entertain guests, interact with doctors, and perform calendrical and family rituals.

In introducing the student to her world the host mother transforms cultural knowledge into personal knowledge for the student. In this process she not only makes her world real to the student, she often unknowingly, but repeatedly, presents to the student the complexities, ambiguities and situatedness of everyday life. The densities of our shared cultural worlds require this kind of a tutelage. Local people provide students with natural hierarchies of highly situated interpretive tasks. Well-crafted study abroad experiences also provide students with access to the relatively unguarded emotions of such people as the language teacher and the host mother. The first of these teaches students how to weight their knowledge of impersonal codes. The second teaches them how to care about these codes. Together they teach students that codes—far from being neutral instruments—are constitutive of human landscapes. They also lead to the ultimate goal of study abroad: a rite of passage through which the student comes to learn that local people are every bit as genuine and complex as the ones he or she left at home. This process, when it works, naturalizes within the student the beginnings of a new lifeworld, one that originally was exotic and alien.

Finally, students are beckoned back to these worlds. This is no doubt because of the density of these worlds, their compelling quality, and the fact that much of the learning a foreign student accomplishes is brokered through personal relations with particular others. Japan in particular appears to draw back large numbers of study-abroad participants following graduation. Anecdotally, it appears that often more than half of any given group of students will return to Japan within three years of graduation, often to stay for an extended period. This is fortunate given the time commitments necessary to acquire high levels of proficiency in the language. While students do progress tremendously in their understanding of the new language and culture on study abroad sojourns, with few exceptions, the density of these cultures requires repeated sojourns for a person to approach being fully "at home."

Challenges

This section presents a list of challenges suggestive of those likely to be encountered by educational institutions as they create or participate in study abroad programs in Asia. It should be noted that many institutions have already responded to these challenges and that their responses provide ready models for others to turn to for guidance.

If the above arguments, or other similar ones, are persuasive, then providing opportunities for liberal arts students to encounter and learn to perform within very different cultures and languages should be seen as a curricular goal of the liberal arts college. From this follow several considerations.

Institutional Development Plan

Asia presents a staggering array of cultures, languages, and histories. With over half the world's population, Asia and the Pacific region also boast more than half the world's extant languages, some 3,000 of them. Of the 25 most widely spoken languages in the world, 16 are found primarily in Asia. The crises of modernity, ideology, and capitalism have reshuffled, and continue to reshuffle, social landscapes throughout Asia. Such diversities provide American colleges and universities with rich opportunities for curricular and institutional development. Asia, unfortunately, has few natural champions within such institutions. Taken together these facts underline the importance of well-conceived institutional development plans.

In putting together a plan an institution must be concerned with a variety of familiar issues, including the provision of adequate language instruction at the home campus before and after sojourns abroad, the staffing of core courses for majors, and the incorporation of Asian materials into courses throughout the curriculum. It is particularly important to avoid responses that settle for relegating Asia and study in Asia to a handful of dedicated faculty and students.

Given the dimensions of these tasks, an institution must also be concerned with maintaining a high profile for such efforts over a long period of time. Faculty development and expansion are an essential part of this process. Supported by the Henry Luce Foundation, ASIANetwork has already worked with many colleges across the United States to formulate long-term institutional development plans to achieve these goals. Recent works also suggest strategies for expanding the home campus curriculum to respond to the challenges posed by students going on and returning from study abroad.[22]

If creative learning at the undergraduate level is best carried on by a learning community, and if the faculty of liberal arts colleges compose an experienced resource for doing this, then as the Asian curriculum of a college expands, it is natural for the social linkages between the college and comparable institutions to expand. To build on its strengths the residential liberal arts college should formulate a long-term development plan with a goal of creating a dense stratified community of learners and educators incorporating local people in Asia, and the faculty and staff of collaborating institutions in Asia, as well as their own students, faculty, and staff.

Perhaps the single biggest impediment to study in Asia for American college students is their own reluctance to get in line. Few students wake up each morning thinking they could learn to speak fluent Chinese or Thai. Yet, many study abroad programs appropriately require language study in the first or second year of college before students go abroad. This means that high school understandings of the world tend to shape the demographics of study abroad, especially in Asia. Recruiting students actively should be a key institutional goal.

Characteristics of On-Site Education

No faculty are trained as experts in study abroad. As a field, study abroad is not part of graduate curricula, with the exception of relatively new programs in the United States largely for administrators.

The premise of on-site cultural immersion is the significant difference in background and daily assumptions between students and local peoples. Since this will always spring from the particular backgrounds of those students and local peoples, and since these continually evolve through time, the field is one that will always have a significant emergent quality. The challenge to faculty is to link this emergent quality to the discourses and insights of their disciplines.

Local faculty teaching study abroad students need to develop ways to bridge four sets of experiences: (1) their own formative experience usually growing up in the field site, successfully passing through its educational institutions, and often going on for some form of advanced study in an English-speaking country; (2) the students' formative experience growing up "abroad," (3) the students' current experience on site, and (4) the experiences of local people with whom the students come into contact.

In working with students, local faculty who are successful in study abroad come to know how to adjust their own language, lesson plans, and assumptions to this special audience. This is often a long-term learning process. Team teaching with faculty from the students' home institutions is an important method for speeding up this process.

Few faculty study pedagogy in their graduate training. Those coming to liberal arts colleges often need to make significant adjustments to become successful teachers. The same is true of study abroad faculty. This is not to suggest that there is a preferred style of teaching; there are surely multiple preferred styles. Rather it is to suggest that effective teaching reaches students and challenges them to think deeply. Teaching is a mode of speaking, and attention to message, context, and receiver is essential.

For students the richness of study in Asia springs from the convergence of the three proficiencies they must acquire: (1) those of the academy in their home countries (they must learn to speak with students and faculty who do not follow them to their study abroad locale), (2) those of the academy in their Asian field site (while faculty should adjust their methods to the background of their students, they ultimately should introduce their foreign and local students to what they see as the best available discourses), and (3) those of everyday life in the Asian locality. This is a multilayered learning task characterized by hybridity and a close attention to situated ways of knowing.

It should be stressed that study abroad is distinct from regular course work at a foreign institution where the student is expected to conform as closely as possible to local standards. The focus on bridging the lifeworlds of the student and the local people means that curricular, cocurricular, and extracurricular activities are often equally educational. Indeed, much of the best education comes in dorms and homestays as students become involved in the lives of local peoples.

This blending of formal and informal educational processes is perhaps study abroad's most important characteristic. It poses one of the central challenges of mounting an effective program. Much of such extracurricular learning should be left to the student. Yet faculty should be encouraged to explore multiple ways of turning students into active learners. Host families, local students, and local institutions can all play important roles in coaching students, answering questions, and providing opportunities for students to engage in research projects. A host of methods have been developed to encourage students to reflect on experiences. These include structured fieldwork assignments, journals, reflective assignments, critical event summaries, and the like. To the extent that such opportunities are not present, students will have a tendency to miss much of what is occurring in front of them.

As possible, local faculty should be aware of the curricular interests and pedagogical styles at the students' home campuses. Study abroad provides to students credit that they use to graduate from their home colleges. For this reason alone there is need for periodic consultations between faculty and administrators in the Asian and American institutions as well as feedback loops from students to both of these groups. These ensure the long-term success of programs.

The pacing of cultural learning, and the time students and institutions commit to it, is also a key variable. Long-term sojourns appear to be much more effective than short-term ones in providing opportunities for students to recognize and settle into the rhythms of daily life. Term or semester programs are often consumed by transitions—the transition to living in the field site, the transition to beginning to recognize local people as individuals rather than as representatives of a foreign culture, the transition to planning for returning home and acquiring gifts for parents and friends. Semester programs provide little time for students to plant roots, to ground themselves in the field site. In a recent National Association for Foreign Student Affairs (NAFSA) meeting it was suggested that the field of study abroad would be well served to develop typologies of different kinds of programs, with the length of sojourn being a key variable.[23]

Finally, it is worth stressing that study abroad is a labor-intensive field. It is a field where caretakers are often the most valuable educators. The density of learning environments requires adequate staffing. For example, to whom does a student turn to learn how to say "shoestrings" in Indonesian, or to inquire about what kinds of stores sell shoestrings, or to ask where the nearest store is located? At a deeper level, to whom does a student turn to discuss why a friend did not show up when he said he would, or why a host mother is becoming withdrawn, or why the student does not "feel good"? It is easy for students to be overwhelmed by the differences they encounter. For this reason, it is best that programs provide a high ratio of staff per student.

Collaboration: Faculty and Staff Development

A significant symmetry characterizes the positions of faculty and staff at Asian institutions and American institutions collaborating on study abroad. The American college has great need for developing its Asia-related curriculum and faculty competencies. The Asian institution has an equally important need to develop the international competencies of its faculty and staff. In both cases these needs are broadly recognized. In both cases, however, institutions have been built and activities routinized along lines that make it difficult to respond to such needs.

Fulbright and other foundations have created programs for supporting faculty exchanges. Study abroad programs, conceived as institutional linkages meant to serve entire institutions, offer another and more predictable opportunity for doing this. The administrative challenge is to expand the vision of study abroad from simply the flow of American students to an Asian location to that of an institutional partnership with both sides exploring how they might complement the needs of the other.

Ideally institutions collaborating in study abroad would also discuss all the following:

- The exchange of students in both directions.
- Faculty exchanges, including team teaching of courses on the field site in Asia as well as at the American campus. Such teaching would build on the complementary competencies of faculty and need not be limited to Asia-related topics.
- Visiting-faculty research projects that provide training and, as possible, credit to local student assistants.
- Short-term programs for visiting faculty and guest lecturers.
- The exchange of teaching assistants and staff members.

The needs of the U.S. college faculty, both Asia specialists and those new to teaching about Asia, should be centrally addressed in formulating these linkages. The challenges confronting Asia specialists in liberal arts colleges tend to be poorly understood by most institutions. Once specialists begin teaching they rarely have opportunities for broad-gauged, relatively unfocused, but lengthy experiences abroad. For U.S. faculty, graduate training often involves sojourns of only a year or two in the Asian country they study. The cultural and linguistic densities referred to earlier mean that many college faculty members, while they are well aware of their personal limitations, are on a career track that does not serve them, or the field of Asian studies, well. The sabbatical-year research model tends to narrow faculty interests just as faculty members develop the tools to begin to grapple with the larger complexities of the Asian world. Asian faculty teaching about the United States face similar challenges. Exchanges provide an important way to enable faculty to deepen and broaden their competencies.

Student Issues

Both liberal inquiry and study abroad have been presented above in idealized terms. This can be helpful in clarifying goals, but we should be careful not to idealize our students or ourselves. Study abroad dislocates and disequilibrates students and faculty. Anyone familiar with study abroad knows that this is true and that, for particular individuals, it can be profoundly upsetting.

It is important not to assume our students are a constant we take abroad. Rather we should approach them much as we approach another cultural setting—as densely structured by conventions needing interpretation for ourselves as well as to local faculty and staff. Students' expectations of themselves, their college years, and study abroad have all been shaped by the conventions of their upbringing. These compose much of the interpretive material, and many of the issues they bring with them to the field site in Asia. One of the key issues many bring is a bias toward personal exploration. They are empiricists: seeing is believing. This comprises much of the popular rationale for studying abroad. College students have reached an age at which they are encouraged to see themselves as disembedded from social formations. In fact, "disembedding" provides an important rationale for the liberal arts college. The college years are often spoken of as a time for exploration, for "serious" play, for the "discovery" of self. Much of this conflicts with the notion that in going abroad one learns through participant observation, through entering into multiple social entanglements.

Understanding such narrative conventions—and discussing them with students—makes it easier both for students to understand the process they are moving through and for faculty elsewhere to speak to the condition of our students. Little, if anything, in their prior education has prepared them for the kind of learning processes they will encounter in Asia. In their prior education learning was highly guided and impersonal. On study abroad much of their most important learning will occur at unpredictable moments and they will have to have the "savvy" to capture such fleeting experiences and pursue what lessons they offer.

As our students enter new landscapes they will often face unexpected challenges. One of these concerns their own language. Most classes for study abroad students in Asia are offered in English. This is unavoidable given the amount of learning required of our students before they acquire high levels of proficiency in an Asian language. Instructors tend to be local scholars who are quite proficient in English as a second language. Our students tend to come from monolingual backgrounds, so they have had little experience working with second-language speakers. Liberal arts students and institutions tend to prefer discussion-oriented classes characterized by complex speech events. In such settings students are often rewarded not for recognizing what was said but for racing ahead to capture implications of what has not yet been said. When they study in Asia they need to slow down to hear what is being said, to recognize that arguments might not be structured along familiar lines and that key vocabulary is likely to be weighted differently. In all these ways they need to develop their "interlingual" English skills. With practice students learn to replace the assumed transparencies of language with opaqueness. They learn that much of the knowledge they acquire on study abroad will come from working across languages, both what they assumed was their own language and the language of the field site.

Taken together these realities mean that students often are unprepared for the hard work of second cultural acquisition, of studying abroad. Predeparture orientations provide an important method for encouraging students to recognize the challenges they will encounter. Continuing orientations throughout the study abroad period are of central importance. It is essential to provide for students on study abroad a thick human interface, one incorporating colearners, advanced learners—including the faculty from their home institutions—as well as local people, faculty, and staff.

Not all our students are up to the dimensions of this task. It is important to create ways to monitor students while they are in Asia. If their performance does not live up to minimal expectations, they should quickly be sent home. This is one of the most difficult decisions facing professionals in the field; the overall quality of study abroad can only be improved by creating easier channels for reaching such decisions. Study abroad should be among the highest privileges an institution makes available to its students, not a right. Not all students are sufficiently mature to be away from their native land.

Conclusion

More than 6,000 students from hundreds of American institutions participated in study abroad in Asia during the 1996–1997 academic year. These students, those who preceded them, their home institutions, and the receiving institutions in Asia all make up an invaluable set of resources for anyone interested in developing study abroad opportunities in Asia. A variety of guides now exist to direct interested readers to these resources.[24]

The people of Asia and institutions across Asia are among our most valuable resources. This can be illustrated with a brief anecdote from my own experience. I direct a program linking Earlham with Morioka, a regional city in northeastern Japan. Recently I had occasion to visit the city and was more than a little surprised—but on reflection quite pleased —to learn that the "Earlham Road Show" was occurring on the same night. I knew that a local group, composed largely of prior host families in the program, had been organized to aid the program in various ways. I did not know that this group had decided to sponsor a show featuring the wife of a prior participant and the daughter of a local resident, a long-time supporter of the program. Both were accomplished musicians. The city's new performance hall was rented for the evening, and several hundred people attended. The show was a great success.

Other similar incidents of the mingling of the story of the American liberal arts college with those of local peoples and institutions across Asia must exist. It would seem that such shared performances are desirable and that we should do what we can to increase them.

Notes

1. See for example, Edward W. Said, *Orientalism*; Bryan S. Turner, *Orientalism, Postmodernism and Globalism*.

2. See Norman L. Kauffman, Judith N. Martin, and Henry D. Weaver, with Judy Weaver; *Students Abroad, Stangers at Home*; Josef A. Mestenhauser, Gayla Marty, and Inge Steglitz, ed., *Culture, Learning, and the Disciplines*; Volunteers in Asia, *Trans-Cultural Study Guide*.

3. Todd M. Davis, ed., *Open Doors 1997/98*, 11–23.

4. It should be noted that only programs recruiting students from other institutions are listed. This suggests that the total number of programs in Asia is

underreported. In several cases, however, an Asian institution will offer a program sponsored by more than one American institution. In such cases the same program of study in Asia could be listed more than once. The chart is put together from Davis, *Open Doors*; and Sara J. Steen, ed., *Academic Year Abroad 1999/2000*.

5. International Liberal Arts Colleges, *In the International Interest*.

6. *Distinctively American*.

7. George P. Schmidt, *The Liberal Arts College*, 213–17.

8. See Peter J. Gomes, "Affirmation and Adaptation: Values and the Elite Residential College," and Eva T.H. Brann, "The American College as the Place for Liberal Learning."

9. Michael S. McPherson and Morton Owen Schapiro, "Economic Challenges for Liberal Arts Colleges," 48–49.

10. Alexander W. Astin, "How the Liberal Arts College Affects Students," 77.

11. Ibid., 85. See also Richard H. Hersh, "Generating Ideals and Transforming Lives," 181–85.

12. Jean-François Lyotard, *The Postmodern Condition*.

13. Richard D. Lambert, *International Studies and the Undergraduate*, 9–44.

14. Clifford Geertz, *The Interpretation of Cultures*, 3–32.

15. Pierre Bourdieu, *The Logic of Practice*, 52–65.

16. Hans Joas, *The Creativity of Action*, 158.

17. Jerome Bruner, *The Culture of Education*, 184.

18. John Hartman, "Thai Language Learning Framework and Forum," Web site *http://www.seasite.niu.edu/Thai/ThaiLLF/Default.htm#IV*.

19. Brann, "The American College," 162.

20. Ibid., 163

21. Eugene M. Lang, "Distinctively American: The Liberal Arts College," 145.

22. Barbara B. Burn, *Integrating Study Abroad into the Undergraduate Liberal Arts Curriculum*.

23. Lilli Engle and John Engle, "Study Abroad Levels."

24. *Peterson's Study Abroad 1998*; Steen, *Academic Year Abroad 1999/2000*. Various Web sites are now devoted to study abroad listings. See Studyabroad.com at *http://www.studyabroad.com*; Petersons.com, The Study Abroad Channel, *http://www.petersons.com/stdyabrd/us.html*; Association of Teachers of Japanese, Bridging Project, *http://www.Colorado.EDU/ealld/atj*, then click to the study abroad page and links.

5

Remapping Asian Studies

Rita Smith Kipp

This chapter looks to the future, charting some directions for the development of Asian studies in the liberal arts environment. "Remapping" here designates three kinds of changes, the first of which are theoretical or conceptual. Our curricula and our teaching should be informed by two significant shifts: critiques of metageographical categories and new ways of conceptualizing culture. Students should understand that "Asia" as well as its regions are constructs that reflect specific histories and political relations. They should see, too, that cultural knowledge flows across mapped boundaries and is not uniformly shared within communities. Above all, cultural knowledge is not biologically heritable.

At a second level, remapping Asian studies refers to a complex of institutional and personal adjustments. As described in more detail in other chapters, the institutional shape of Asian studies has not been static, for it has changed in response to geopolitical shifts as well as larger trends in higher education. In recent decades, Asian studies has become more dispersed, adapting itself to a new educational terrain, the liberal arts environment. ASIANetwork deliberately encourages this adaptive radiation. This new institutional niche differs in significant ways from the research universities where Asian studies first appeared and where most of the Asianists now teaching in liberal arts colleges were trained. Focusing on the goal of liberal education and on the relationship of Asian studies to humanistic study, newly minted Asianists may need to "remap" their goals as teachers and scholars. They will feel the tension between maintaining their hard-won expertise as specialists and making that expertise useful and interesting for students, most of whom will not themselves become scholars or area specialists. Asian studies at the undergraduate level is an essential component of a humane literacy that equips our students, regardless of their career paths, to understand better a diverse and interconnected world community, and to live more fully in it.

Finally, the term "remapping" will be used only briefly here in a quite prosaic and literal sense to argue for bringing maps, and the study of geography, back into the classroom. Maps will come into our classrooms increasingly via electronic media. More significantly, determining what maps mean, and how to read them, requires a critical perspective about maps as artifacts and about the purposes of mapping, an argument that circles back to the idea of remapping our theories and concepts.

The Myth of Asia and Other Places

Few books have influenced scholarship on Asia as much as Edward Said's *Orientalism.*[1] Said argued that European scholarship and travel literatures had constructed a timeless and exotic "East" (a vague expanse of cultural territory extending from the Arab world to Japan) as the "Other" against which Europe understood itself as consisting of world conquerors. The East-West dichotomy remains prevalent in lectures, classroom discussions, and new publications. The East, characterized by religious sensibilities, familial social orders, and ageless traditions, contrasts with the West, supposedly impelled by rationality, material and technical dynamism, and individualism. Nationalist intelligentsia in the colonial world appropriated this gross schema, and even today leaders still use it, often for their own political ends in contrasting themselves to outsiders.[2] When Malaysia's Muhamad Matahir or Singapore's Lee Kuan Yew speak of Asian values, they employ this kind of dichotomous framework.

Because the East-West dualism keeps being reinvented in scholarly as well as popular discourse, deconstructing it remains a goal in Asian studies classrooms more than twenty years after *Orientalism* was published. Consider, for example, David Landes's *The Wealth and Poverty of Nations: Why Some Are So Rich and Others So Poor*, a tome that describes 1,000 years of world economic history. Landes, an emeritus professor at Harvard, arrives at the conclusion that Western culture and values, especially as the English embody these, underlie the West's technological and economic ascendency.[3] Like scholars in other disciplines, especially sociology, Landes seeks to explain Western exceptionalism, that is, what was different about the European trajectory of development. One of Landes's critics, Andre Gunder Frank, argues that European economic development is only exceptional if one's historical purview is limited to the past several hundred years. In *ReOrient: Global Economy in the Asian Age*, Frank shows that globalization has ancient roots, and that China was long the fulcrum of the world economy.[4] Like Frank, anthropologist Jack Goody finds that "the superior achievements of the West can no longer be seen as permanent or even longstanding features of those cultures but as the result of one of the swings of the pendulum that has affected these societies over the millennia."[5] A truly global understanding of world history and economic change, however, ultimately requires our putting aside a posture of the East versus the West, and coming to terms with the complex and ancient interrelatedness of the world. As Frank's work (and that of other scholars) shows, any portrayal of European history as sui generis, as if economic and cultural relations with China, India, the Arab world, and Southeast Asia were merely incidental to a largely indigenous transformation, will have missed an important formative dynamic of world history.[6]

Today those who teach Asian studies in colleges and universities, many of them trained as specialists of a particular Asian time and place, are appropriately wary about using "the East" or "the Orient." At the same time, in our classrooms and other scholarly discourse, "the West" or "Western" still turns up often as the comparison point for topics of discussion in various specific Asian traditions. A term such as "the West" homogenizes and essentializes that entity (just as there is no unitary East, there is no West that is not also differentiated into specifically local traditions, urban and rural life ways, working class and elite, men and women, and so on) and logically implies an East, even if one never uses that term.[7] Expunging this dualistic global usage is very hard if not impossible, but at the very least these ubiquitous terms and their essentializing implications need to be addressed deliberately at some point in every undergraduate classroom where the subject involves Asia. If we cannot rid ourselves of this all too handy dualism, we can at least educate our students to be nervous about using it, and alert them to mind the rhetorical context whenever they encounter it in their own or others' language.

East and West are only the largest of the metageographical constructs under fire in *The Myth of Continents: A Critique of Metageography*, an important book by Martin Lewis and Kären Wigen, a geographer and a historian respectively. As the title suggests, the book takes aim at the idea that there are seven continents that equate to the world's major land masses. The most mythical of the continents are surely Asia and Europe. Determining where the hypothetical dividing line is on this great continuum has long been a point of contention, but this is not Lewis and Wigen's concern. They point out that designating Europe as a continent at all elevates its visibility on the world stage, as if its small land area were of equal conceptual weight to terrestrial giants such as Africa and South America. In fact, most of the other modes of "mythical" thinking that these two scholars explode are, like this notion of continents, ways of thinking about and mapping Europe so that conceptually its peoples and history rise first in our minds. They argue that European maps and atlases, and ways of comparing Europe to other places in the world, consistently make that area larger than life.[8]

The question of where Europe stops and Asia begins, and of whether Europe deserves to be termed a continent, leads Lewis and Wigen to question also whether Asia is a useful category at all. They determine that it is not. Like other scholars before them, to whom they give credit, Lewis and Wigen organize the world's terrain into cultural and historical regions rather than land forms. In Lewis and Wigen's world regions, "There is no logically constituted geographical category called Asia."[9] In fact, of all the so-called continents, "Asia is not only the largest but also the most fantastically diversified, a vast region whose only commonalities—whether human or physical—are so general as to be trivial."[10]

This nonentity, Asia, is a conceptual artifact of twentieth-century politics, as is the institutional edifice called Asian studies, composed of professional associations, granting agencies' categories, academic programs, and professional journals that emerged in response to World War II and the Cold War.[11] Even so, "Asia" cannot be easily conjured away, even by Lewis and Wigen themselves, who utilize that term in no fewer than five of the fourteen world regions into which they carve the globe—Central Asia, South Asia, Southwest Asia and North Africa, Southeast Asia, and East Asia. These familiar divisions largely correspond to those recognized in the Association for Asian Studies and other institutional settings and are the categories that Asianists themselves typically use to name their own expertise.[12] Lewis and Wigen use "Asia" in these labels as a mere convention, not to denote fragments of something larger. But just as "the West" logically creates its antithesis, these regional names will continue to reproduce "Asia" by implication, even if, geographically or culturally speaking, there is no larger conceptual umbrella under which all the sub-Asias can be reasonably grouped. Like the East-West dichotomy, then, Asia is not going to go away, because it is a myth we keep reproducing in both our everyday and scholarly discourses.

Even more common than continent and region in academic and journalistic discourse is the metageographical unit of the nation-state. Because the nation-state so frequently defines and limits our scholarship and course content, we need to pay special attention to the way this category often seduces our thinking and that of our students.[13] Almost always, students taking their first course about China, India, Japan, or other Asian nation-states will not anticipate the extent to which these entities are composed of people speaking diverse languages and living diverse lives, whether divided along ethnic and religious lines, or along lines of gender, class, and other dimensions. Indeed, complicating what "India" or "China" means to students is surely one of our most basic tasks as teachers in Asian studies.

One place to start complicating matters is by heightening students' awareness of the distinction between the state—a set of related but distinguishable organizations that concentrate power—and the nation, an "imagined community," in Benedict Anderson's famous phrase.[14] States are not "natural and fundamental building blocks of global geography," but, rather, "constructed, contingent, and often imposed political-geographical units."[15] Along these lines, Thongchai Winichakul's *Siam Mapped: A History of the Geo-Body of a Nation* argues that "The geo-body of a nation is merely an effect of modern geographical discourse whose prime technology is a map."[16] Thai cosmography and an indigenous way of conceptualizing state power as center defined rather than boundary circumscribed gave way, in nineteenth-century Thailand, when up against European cartography and an imagined *world* divided among territorially bounded, mutually exclusive nation-states. A historian, Thongchai shows what difference this geopolitical shift makes in the interpretation of Thai history, finding that the histories and perspectives of non–Thai-speaking peoples, especially those at the margins of the region's nation-states, get elided between the telos of Bangkok's rise and the story of French colonial imperialism.

Historians, indigenous as well as foreign, have so frequently defined their subject as the linear story of the nation-state that some recent scholars now plead that history needs to be rescued from the nation.[17] Although state and nation are commonly wedded in a single hyphenated term these days, in relatively few instances are state and nation perfectly coterminous. While nationalist histories depict the sovereign state as a spontaneous outcome of that imagined fraternity that is the nation, a causal arrow extends also in the reverse direction. That is, the state deploys resources to create, strengthen, or reproduce the nation. Katherine Bowie's account of an emotional ritual of incorporation into Thailand's right-wing Village Scouts movement and Sheldon Garon's book about the management of morality and national loyalty in Japan are two recent descriptions of Asian states expending considerable effort to reproduce the nation.[18]

Interrogating Culture

The metageographical units (world regions) through which Lewis and Wigen limn the world's cultural and historical diversity have, in turn, their own heuristic limitations. With the exception of Southeast Asia, which has a certain residual quality, all the other world regions in their schema supposedly have "inherent unique personalities" deriving from shared historical processes.[19] Like the old idea of continents, their world regions device "implies that the map of the world is readily divisible into a small number of fundamentally comparable units."[20] Their schema suggests, too, that there is a high degree of shared features within regions (that is, cultural similarities), and that peoples and ideas stay more or less put in them. Phenomena such as migration and diasporas, international trade in films and music, and other globalizing forces wreak havoc, however, on anyone's regional mapping of cultures. Cultures are no longer *places*, Lewis and Wigen admit: "In effect, the geography of social life in the late twentieth century has outgrown . . . the very conventions by which we represent spatial patterns in image and text."[21]

In an essay published in a special issue of *Daedalus* on the meaning of being Chinese today, Harvard philosopher Tu Wei-ming attempted to chart the boundaries of "cultural China." He delineated three interacting symbolic universes, each of which defies contiguous mapping in any geographic sense: Mainland China, in which he includes Singapore (!) and Taiwan; people of Chinese descent in diaspora over the entire world; and a scholarly community—teachers, journalists, and others—who read and write about China, regardless of their racial or ethnic heritage. Together, these three spatially discontinuous universes comprise "cultural China." Tu stresses the extent to which these universes communicate and interact, influencing and reacting to each other:

> For the last decades the international discourse on cultural China has unquestionably been shaped by the third symbolic universe more than by the first two combined. Specifically, writing in English and in Japanese

have had a greater impact on the intellectual discourse on cultural China than those written in Chinese.[22]

Placing cultural China on a map, any map, would seem impossible in these terms. Tu's dilemma of how to locate "cultural China" may defy any mappable solution, but China as an imperial power in the past and as a contemporary state can well be mapped, and China's shifting and contested boundaries—in Tibet, Taiwan, the Spratleys, and elsewhere—can well be brought forward for discussion in classes about history and politics. The point is to teach students both the differences and the *relationships* between the mapped (the state) and the unmappable (the culture and the nation).

What "cultural" means is equally as problematic as where "China" is. In the United States, the culture concept has been central to that variegated discipline called anthropology, always an ambitious but increasingly unwieldy conglomerate that encompasses studies of prehistory, human evolution, and linguistics, as well as contemporary cultural variation. Although anthropologists have never fully agreed about how, exactly, to define culture, debates about their discipline's supposedly centripetal concept have risen to new heights in recent decades. Some anthropologists, writing "against culture," have argued that the term is so fraught with problems it is best to avoid using it; others, while recognizing its limitations, wish to retain it for practical purposes.[23] Some anthropologists are comfortable using only the adjectival form, "cultural," avoiding the noun altogether.

The new unease and caution about this term mark an important shift that has implications far beyond the squabbling among professional anthropologists, who, after all, do not own the culture concept. On the contrary, a quasi-anthropological sense of the term is far more pervasive today than it was when I began teaching twenty-three years ago. Then, I always devoted some time in my introductory classes to differentiating an anthropological sense of the term from some everyday uses that described culture as something that came in analogical quantities, implying that some individuals could be highly cultured while others were not. Today, the common everyday sense of the term *is* an anthropological sense, and one not restricted just to describing ethnic groups or whole societies. We speak easily now of corporate cultures, for example, or comment on the different cultures of college campuses. Culture, like Asia and the East-West dichotomy, will not soon disappear from the vocabulary of anthropologists and other scholars, in part because our students increasingly carry the term into our classrooms.

As "culture" has increasingly entered our mundane conceptual repertoire, however, anthropologists have become disturbed to see it used increasingly, too, as part of an arsenal in exclusionary rhetoric based on what has been called cultural fundamentalism, a kind of "racism without race."[24] Calls for tighter immigration policies in Europe or the horrors of ethnic cleansing come to mind. It is probably no accident that identity politics reemerged with new vigor (and virulence) in the latter half of the twentieth century, precisely as the flow of information and ideas, as well as persons, across national boundaries increased in volume and frequency. Hybridity of minds as well as bodies confuses the older, comfortable categories through which we understand ourselves and others, prompting some to rebuild or reinforce whenever possible those clarifying conceptual bulwarks between ideally pure races and hypothetically distinct cultures.

Verena Stolcke comments that "This cultural rhetoric is distinct from racism in that it reifies culture conceived as a compact, bounded, localized, and historically rooted set of traditions and values transmitted through the generations."[25] My own experiences with students' language in the classroom suggest, however, that this notion of essentialized cultures is not very far from racism after all. Observe the way students and others frequently speak as if the boundaries of cultures were set by the physical ancestry of persons, that is, as if the term "culture" designated ethnic *groups*, societies, or people in some other form. For example, the so-called heritage student has increasingly entered Asian studies classrooms expressing the desire to learn about her culture. Clearly she does not mean the language she grew up speaking (English) or the lifestyle almost indistinguishable from that of her high school classmates in her Cincinnati suburb, that is, her language and culture as an ethnographer might study them. Rather, she means the language and history of Korea or Japan, as if her culture were *hers by virtue of genealogy.* In their exams and essays, my students often slip into usages equating a culture with a bounded group of persons, or reifying it as a sentient agent. A bright senior major in my department was writing recently about how archaeologists sometimes get drawn into nationalistic disputes or other claims about territory, valuables, and resources: "If recognized archaeological cultures are assumed to correspond to modern cultures," she wrote, "the modern cultures can use this to lay claim to the land, because they say that they have always been there, so the land should not be taken away from them." A culture—if understood as an abstraction standing for shared ways of speaking, acting, and thinking—can never "lay claim to the land." The student's linguistic slip, a shorthand way of speaking of a group of people who perhaps share some ways of thinking and acting (or in this case, at least, share a political claim) as if *they* were a culture, is very common indeed, and even anthropologists sometimes commit this linguistic slip.

Is this a hair worth splitting? It is, and precisely because of the very conflicts and claims this student was attempting to analyze. Identity politics arise around disputes about land, jobs, sacred relics, or other treasures, as well as about intangible goods such as dignity and political representation. Such disputes are difficult enough to resolve without participants holding racist presumptions that tend to foreclose dialogue and interaction. An imprecise way of speaking about culture as if it were synonymous with persons does not provide the conceptual tools to think our way around the difficult issues of race, a task fully as important in Asian studies classrooms as in American studies classrooms. Race matters, not only because the world is shrinking and our communities are increasingly diverse, but also because so much of the history of twentieth-century Asia was shaped around this issue. The colonial project, as much recent scholarship has shown, built a thoroughly racial edifice, although its contours varied from colonial power to colonial power and from place to place.[26] Understanding the rise of nationalism in Asia is hardly possible without understanding the contradictions between the Enlightenment values of democracy and equality that nationalists such as Ho Chi Minh and others learned from their European educations, and the interpersonal slights and institutional barriers they suffered as a consequence of racial categorizing.[27] The liberationist rhetoric of Japan during World War II, which cultivated racial sentiments, rallying Asians against Europeans, thus fell on ground well prepared by European colonial practices.

The position of minorities in Japan, the violence perpetrated against the Chinese during every political crisis in Indonesia, racial tensions in American cities—one does not have to look far to show that racism is by no means merely a historical curiosity. The religious studies department at your college wins the chance to recruit for a position in Hinduism or South Asian religions. Must the successful applicant be someone of Indian descent? Baby girls from China have been adopted by Canadian and American families in large numbers since the advent of China's one-child policy. How do these families respond to the ethical charge that cross-racial adoptions deprive children of their culture?[28] Neither of these is merely a hypothetical issue, of course, and issues such as these will no doubt continue to arise, challenging us to think through the link between culture and race again and again. Sorting carefully through terms such as race, culture, and society—terms that occur frequently in our classrooms regardless of discipline—is important in Asian studies classrooms because students need to understand and negotiate the identity politics that are ubiquitous in our lives.

Franz Boas, a Jewish immigrant from Germany who established anthropology in the American academy in the early twentieth century, was instrumental in the careful parsing of race, culture, and language that occurred in that discipline.[29] Boas accorded culture and language the lion's share of explanatory value in accounting for human behavior, while clarifying that in humans behaviors are overwhelmingly learned, not inborn. Some recent critics feel that Boas, however much he downplayed race as an explanatory tool, still understood race to be those "objective" biological differences among humans, differences amenable to scientific study.[30] In contrast, some anthropologists have now discarded race altogether as a useful heuristic, viewing the term instead as a folk concept or social construction, albeit one with enormous consequences. Biological or physical anthropologists are more likely to speak of populations than races, or to use other biologically neutral concepts to describe human physical and genetic variation.

More has changed in the culture concept than the parsing of race from culture. Because culture is about *shared* ideas and ways of behaving, the concept leads us to overlook fundamental disagreements within a society, fundamental contradictions within a culture. Beginning in the mid-1970s, feminist critiques within anthropology began to chip away at the idea that cultures are internally homogeneous, or that ideas and ways of behaving are shared uniformly throughout a community. Classic ethnographies, written about *the* Naga or *the* Javanese, were then reread skeptically and found to be based primarily on men's lives, or sometimes primarily on only the opinions and experiences of the senior or elite members of the society. Anthropologists have been wrestling with this, and its implications for ethnographic writing, ever since. One of Clifford Geertz's now classic essays argued that the task of the ethnographer is to understand and translate the "native's point of view."[31] Of late the question has become, which native? And how many?[32] Ideas and practices, rather than shared uniformly within certain bounded social groups, are differentially distributed. Lars Rodseth explains that "[E]ach individual, even in a small-scale society, carries but a portion of his or her 'culture,' and views that culture from a unique social and semantic position."[33] The proposition that no two persons share exactly the same repertoire of values, behaviors, and opinions produces a "Rashoman effect," says Christoph Brumann, referring to the famous Kurosawa film that retells a single event (a rape) from four different vantages. Anthropologists, historians, and other scholars in Asian studies face this kind of dilemma in deciding what the content of a particular culture is, or at least how to write about it.

The distribution of cultural elements is not altogether random, however.[34] When we locate a practice or value within something called "Vietnamese culture," students should understand that this practice or value probably has other coordinates worth noting, a class location, perhaps, or one defined by region or gender. The production and reproduction of any cultural form should always be taken as problematic. *Whose* value or practice is it, and why does it seem to us, and perhaps to many Vietnamese too, as diagnostic or typical, whereas other things we observe in Vietnam are relegated to a secondary, irrelevant, or even deviant designation? Why is the Confucian tradition in Vietnam somehow more diagnostic or definitive than the myriad ways in which it was and is contested or flaunted in word and in everyday practice? "Symbolic production," the late Roger Keesing reminded us, "is linked to power and interest."[35] Teaching about cultures as internally homogeneous sets of ideas and practices occludes this insight about power and ill prepares our students to apprehend critically the politics of culture unfolding all around them.

This perspective, that cultural elements are differentially distributed and always implicated with power, should be communicated to students in Asian studies classrooms where casual uses of the term "culture" often take sharedness for granted. Qualifying and complicating these everyday senses of culture is also part of the challenge of teaching area studies. Teaching about Asian cultures, we find that our role, once again, requires making the initially simple increasingly complex. Although students may enter our classrooms imagining cultures as little boxes inside which things are uniformly shared, we can lead them to understand cultures as sets of arguments, arenas of dispute. Our goal should be to understand the terms of those arguments. Writers and teachers go about this in different ways. Neil Jamieson's *Understanding Vietnam*, for example, tries to dispel any sense of a unified Vietnamese culture by talking about the terms that encapsulate the significant disagreements, contradictions, and inconsistencies within this tradition and within Vietnamese society.[36] Confucian privileging of males and of patrilineal bonds coexists with bilateral tendencies in kin terminology, legends about women warriors, and a strong predilection for stories of romance that defy Confucian obligations. Buddhist ideals of compassionate non-attachment vie with other values that attach people firmly to each other through webs of love and obligation as kin.

The culture concept, when used in a particulate sense to talk about *a* culture, or to compare, say, Japanese to Chinese culture, conveys the idea that cultures are somehow unique, self-contained, and bounded worlds. The stuff of culture, however, has always denoted phenomena that resist encasement. Ideas, values, beliefs, material objects, patterns of behavior—these are not dammed in by mapped boundaries, geographic obstacles, or even social boundaries and social networks. Rather, cultural elements flow across spaces both social and geographic, transforming people's lives while undergoing transformation themselves through persons' practice, use, and creative adaptation of them. One example of this can be found in James L. Watson's edited collection, *Golden Arches East: McDonald's in East Asia.*[37] The contributors show how an icon of the American way of life takes on distinctly local characteristics in Hong Kong, Beijing, and Tokyo, even as it also has various impacts on family life, youth culture, and national identity in these different settings.

Imputing not only homogeneity but easy boundaries to cultural phenomena imputes also an essential and unchanging quality to people's ideas and practices. Culturalist explanations of economic development or the failure to develop, such as that of David Landes mentioned above, tend to "overgeneralize the creative activity," Jack Goody observed, as if everyone were uniformly entrepreneurial or inventive in society X and risk-averse or unmotivated in society Y.[38] Culturalist explanations also attribute causality to culture, as if tradition were a bedrock of practices and values somehow irreducible and immovable.

Samuel Huntington's much discussed book *The Clash of Civilizations and the Remaking of World Order* exemplifies culturalist explanations and their limitations.[39] Dividing the world into six or seven civilizations (depending on whether Africa should be added to a list composed of Sinic, Japanese, Islamic, Hindu, Western, and Latin American traditions), he reasons as follows:

Cultures can change, and the nature of their impact on politics and economics can vary from one period to another. Yet the major differences in political and economic development among civilizations are clearly rooted in their different cultures. East Asian economic success has its source in East Asian culture, as do the difficulties East Asian societies have had in achieving stable democratic political systems. Islamic culture explains in part the failure of democracy to emerge in much of the Muslim world. Developments in the postcommunist societies of Eastern Europe and the former Soviet Union are shaped by their civilizational identities. Those with Western Christian heritages are making progress toward economic development and democratic politics; the prospects for economic and political development in the Orthodox countries are uncertain; the prospects in the Muslim republics are bleak.[40]

Robert W. Hefner, an anthropologist, writes against culturalist explanations for economic development as well as for democratic civility. Hefner takes issue with Huntington and others who suppose that civilizations are unitary and resistant to changes. Hefner and his contributors in two recent edited collections work with a "trimmed down" notion of culture and its causal properties. In *Market Cultures: Society and Morality in the New Asian Capitalisms* they do not argue that culture does not matter in economic development. Hefner writes, "To speak of capitalism's embeddedness is to recognize that market processes are everywhere mediated by a host of facilitative structures."[41] Of course, the shapes of these "facilitative structures" differ in their particulars in China, Japan, and the United States. Likewise, Hefner argues in *Democratic Civility: The History and Cross-cultural Possibility of a Modern Political Ideal* that Muslim societies and others outside the European tradition are not precluded from democratic futures by the weight of tradition. Instead, almost every tradition has "undeveloped possibilities," or "low-lying precedents," that can be adapted and retrofitted to forge locally viable democratic civilities.[42]

Countering views of culture that emphasize continuity and stasis, some theorists have worked to conceptualize how cultures change continuously. Putting any idea into words, or producing any material object from a mental model of what we suppose that object *should* look like (what we might call practicing or enacting culture) reproduces and simultaneously risks that idea or that mental model. The stuff of culture is thus constantly being modified and reworked in the mundane practices of everyday life.[43] Change is often imperceptibly gradual, but al-

ways continuous. Long ago, Charles Hockett provided a clear and eloquent explanation of how this same kind of gradual change operates in
languages as well. [44]

Students will enter a course on Chinese history, or on cultures of
Southeast Asia, *expecting* a bounded geographical phenomenon, however the teacher decides to lump or split it, and *expecting* to gain a sense
of the cultural stuff comprising it. They should leave these courses understanding the problems of drawing boundaries, and of how boundaries shift through time and according to the perspective from which
one draws them. They should come to appreciate that the cultural "stuff"
consists, not of easy laundry lists, but of a range of debates and conflicts
in which some positions were or are more privileged than others, thus
appearing definitive until we look more deeply. Finally, they should see
that the diversity and conflicts that characterize any particular historical
moment provide us, too, with a sense of the dynamics of change in that
moment. Who "won" particular arguments at that time and why? How
does the diversity in that moment foreshadow later patterns of change
and diversity? From this perspective, Asian traditions, both in the past
and the present, should appear more like shifting kaleidoscopes than
essential bedrocks.

Decentering Asian Studies: The Undergraduate Terrain

Asian studies in the United States developed mostly through institutional structures that funneled resources to a limited number of centers
and large research universities.[45] The Department of Defense was a major patron of Asian language study for many years. The geopolitical
interests of the United States, it was argued, were served by educating
experts whose research would inform foreign policy and whose knowledge could be tapped when necessary. Universities competed for grants
under the Department of Education to establish and maintain area studies centers. Those who could not come up with coherent programs and
verify their educational productivity lost their funding. Many Asianists
now teaching in the academy are products of these federally funded
centers, and even Asianists who were trained elsewhere have often used
these centers for summer language study or stints of library research.

While these centers continue to perpetuate and benefit Asian studies
in important ways, in recent decades a number of things have occurred
to undermine this system, ranging from the end of the Cold War and a

reduction in federal spending for higher education to critiques from within the academy itself. Some of these critiques began as intradisciplinary struggles over what kind of scholarship counts as the most legitimate and authoritative. Some political scientists, for example, condemn those in their discipline who engage in area studies as being too concerned with parochial details at the expense of theory and comparison. Economists, too, who presume that human economic behavior is universally comprehensible, have often advised younger colleagues not to get too drawn into area studies, a diversion from their primary intellectual community. At large universities, the "centeredness" of Asian studies creates an interdisciplinary community whose interests compete to some extent with those communities of scholars created within the disciplinary structures, despite the fact that—even at universities with area centers—most faculty holding appointments in Asian studies are hired and housed by the conventional disciplinary departments.

Also during recent decades, the job market in academe entered a major decline from which it has not yet recovered. The centers were graduating more area studies Ph.D.'s than could be absorbed into positions there or at other large research universities. Simultaneously, however, a new educational niche opened—the liberal arts college—where Asian studies continues to enjoy growth. The expansion of Asian studies into undergraduate, largely private, institutions is being spurred no doubt by a number of factors: First, while the locales and the specifics of economic relations constantly change, it is clear that the United States and Asia will remain economically important to each other for an indefinite future; second, and related to this, significant numbers of our students are attracted to studying abroad in Asia and learning Asian languages; and, finally, the middle and upper middle classes, which constitute the main market for liberal arts education, increasingly include Americans of Asian descent.

One implication of this dispersion of Asian studies into the liberal arts terrain is that our educational goals as Asianists must also shift. Just as few of my students at Kenyon College have pursued anthropology as a career, few of them have gone on to become Asianists within the academy. Educating students in Asian studies at our campuses is seldom a matter of reproducing our academic specializations, but rather of helping students acquire a broad base of knowledge and competencies to live a good life. Deciding what *is* a "good life" is, of course, one of the tasks usually set out for students, implicitly or explicitly and early in their careers, at liberal arts colleges. How Asia fits into our students' futures is far from uniform. Some who study about Asia as undergraduates may put their knowledge to use for a few adventurous years of teaching English abroad; others hope to parlay it into a career in international business or foreign relations; most, perhaps, simply use it informally throughout their lives to better understand their coworkers and neighbors, current events, or artistic displays and developments.

Teaching Southeast Asian art history, Stanley O'Connor observed, is an exercise in "humane literacy," an exercise familiar also to those who teach about other regions and other subjects.[46]

> When it is something more than an inert, formal ritual, liberal education is about risking the self so that it may be broadened and deepened, so that it will be rooted fully in its time and place in a way that is effective, responsible, and imaginatively rich. . . . Paradoxically, we study the art of people remote from us in space, time or intellectual habit—in this case Southeast Asia—not because we necessarily wish to take up residence in their fields, village, or cities, or so that we may become friends, but in order that we may live in a more wakeful, mindful and composed way in the adventive present of a world we are actually making.[47]

In short, O'Connor, like most of us who teach about Asia in liberal arts colleges, justifies his teaching to undergraduates neither as a contribution to the geopolitical and defensive interests of the nation, nor to reproduce specialists about Asia in infinite regress as an end in itself. Rather, the educational endeavor O'Connor describes as "risking the self" can hardly be accomplished today without acknowledging and confronting, through disciplined, academic study, the deep diversity, yet interconnectedness, of the human condition. Newspapers and other mass media, the Internet, the arts, and rapid transportation—all the things that make our world smaller, and make it one—have changed what it takes to accomplish effective liberal education from what it took 100 years ago and more, when most American liberal arts colleges were founded. Whatever our students decide living the good life will mean for them, surely it will be lived in a smaller world with diverse others— Muslims, speakers of Hindi or Chinese, Japanese "salary men"—who have come to rather different answers about the good life.

Asian studies is further decentered in the liberal arts setting because so many of our students can and do choose to study abroad for a semester or year during their undergraduate careers. A comparison of fifty liberal arts colleges emphasizing international education found that students in those colleges are three times more likely to study abroad than are students at other kinds of colleges and universities.[48] This is partly a matter of economics. Students who can afford the tuition at these mostly private institutions can also afford to study abroad. Indeed, in view of the cost of attending Kenyon College, study abroad usually represents a significant *savings* for students and their families. Students in Asian studies who elect to study abroad are generally looking to solidify their mastery of languages they have begun to study, or to learn languages—such as Hindi or Indonesian—that are not available on their campuses. Serving as a panelist a few years ago for a granting agency that funds dissertation research in Asia and the Pacific, I was struck by how many of those Ph.D. candidates, compared to graduate students in my day, already had significant experience and well-established contacts in the countries in which they intended to carry out research. For most, this had begun when they were still undergraduates. It is no wonder that liberal arts colleges provide "far more than their reasonable share of the 'seed corn' for efforts in world affairs."[49]

The recent critiques of Asian studies—for carving out artificial geographical units for examination, or as too parochial and insular, not theoretical and comparative enough—are overdrawn. Someone who thinks that scholarship about Asia has been "unaffected by the theoretical and epistemological debates being conducted in the disciplines" has not been following that scholarship.[50] Because I know best the scholarship by Southeast Asianists, I would cite here only Benedict Anderson's *Imagined Communities*, and James Scott's *Weapons of the Weak* and *The Moral Economy of the Peasant*, book titles that have come to be used as veritable codes within and beyond their disciplines, and the work of Clifford Geertz, whose writings shaped a whole generation of anthropologists and reached well beyond anthropology.[51] Critiques about the insularity of Asian studies seem aimed especially at the *centeredness* of the enterprise at large universities, as if these centers were self-sufficient academic subcommunities. In fact, area studies faculty move back and forth between departmental offices and center activities, and those activities (for example, brown bag presentations, symposia, lecture and publication series) are always multidisciplinary if not interdisciplinary.

Certainly in the small colleges and universities that are the membership of ASIANetwork, centered insularity is far less a risk than it may be elsewhere. Many Asian studies programs at these small colleges do not have physical centers at all, but remain merely a way to organize faculty and marshal resources housed in other institutional niches. Furthermore, at liberal arts institutions faculty are generally required to teach a far broader range of courses than they would be asked to do at a large university, so they remain (or grow into) generalists, both within their disciplines and in Asian studies. There are advantages and disadvantages to this situation, as we all know, but one advantage is that we are less likely than those who do not teach outside the circle of their expertise to succumb to what one critic of area studies called an enclosed, self-referential style of scholarship and teaching.[52] Yes, liberal arts faculty also experience the pull between their department and their area or interdisciplinary interests, and almost everywhere administrators wrestle with how to allocate faculty resources to staff area studies and other interdisciplinary programs when the disciplines usually strike a prior claim to those resources. But since—regardless of these territorial quandaries— a common commitment to teaching and to education for *life* mark these campuses, the conflict between disciplinary versus interdisciplinary work exerts less force here than at research universities.

Even if the critiques of area studies are overdrawn, the imperatives of globalization (not to mention the imperatives of minding our own career futures) do mean that in both our scholarship and our teaching Asianists should be doing what we can term "Asian studies plus." That is, our linguistic and locally specific expertise should engage whenever possible with comparative and theoretical projects, an agenda that translates remarkably well to the kind of intellectual demands made on us as generalists in liberal arts settings. At almost all these small colleges, where teaching well is encouraged and rewarded, faculty have also faced increasing pressures to engage in scholarship and to publish, and for many of us that means publishing—and thus remaining in the conversations—within our disciplines. If there was a time when people viewed teaching at the liberal arts college and the research university as divergent career paths, some convergence has recently occurred. These colleges increasingly encourage faculty scholarship, while large universities have been called to account—by the public, politicians, and education leaders—for the quality of teaching and learning. The dispersion of Asianists into the liberal arts environment, along with the concurrent pressures on them to remain active scholar teachers, means that Asianists from liberal arts colleges increasingly populate professional conferences, serve in the professional organizations and on editorial boards, and produce books and articles.

Can we continue to justify *area* studies in the academy anywhere in a world where all boundaries appear constructed and permeable, and where dispersion of people and ideas is the order of the day? Can we still use "culture" to generalize about our own and other ways of life? Having deconstructed East versus West, Asia, culture, and other related terms in scholarly discussions over the last few decades, we still need to teach through and against these terms if only because students bring them into our classrooms. We must continue, too, to make our scholarship comprehensible and interesting to those outside the academy whenever possible. Other terms to substitute for these, should they be invented, would no doubt carry other conceptual entrapments, but understanding this postmodern conundrum of language does not mean we can stop speaking or teaching. Counterposing and qualifying everyday usages and assumptions with critical, scholarly understandings is really at the heart of much humanistic and social scientific education, whether in area studies or in the disciplines.

There are additional implications in terms of how we draw the curricular boundaries in our own syllabi and reading assignments. Like Tu Wei-ming conceptualizing "cultural China," we should be conceptualizing and teaching *cultural* Vietnam, *cultural* India—that is, opening our classrooms to diasporic studies and literatures and bringing these into creative dialogue with literatures and research located in Asia. Teaching about the cultures of Southeast Asia, I have sometimes included books such as *America Is in the Heart: A Personal History*, a mix of fiction and autobiography about Filipino experience in postwar California, and *Emigrants, Entrepreneurs, and Evil Spirits*, an ethnography about a village in the Philippines where circular migration to Hawaii strongly shapes the local economy and social structure.[53] Such inclusions convey the extent to which persons and cultural elements flow back and forth across the world's boundaries, encouraging students to think about change and hybridity.

These conceptual changes in the way we think about geographical categories and about culture also have immediate implications for how we define our programs and our courses. At the programmatic level, many colleges and universities effectively delimit their "Asian" studies to one region or even one country (most often, China), on the reasonable assumption that limited resources can best be deployed in a concentrated fashion. Wittenberg's focus on East Asian Studies, with its undergraduate journal about that region, or Earlham's specialization in the study of Japan, including multiple study abroad options, are exemplars of this strategy of concentration. In other small colleges, the study of Asia may have begun, as it did at Kenyon College, by cobbling together a program from expertise that happened to be at hand and that also happened to represent a wide swath of Asia. In this case, we created a curriculum that encourages broad comparison across Asia, expecting that students will likely specialize in the study of China, Japan, or India but will also take at least one course about another region. Our senior capstone course varies depending on who teaches it, but it always includes a cross-regional and comparative element.

The dilemma of teaching about Asia, an area that has little historical and/or cultural unity, is nowhere more pointed than at the level of the introductory survey course. In the spring of 1998, participants in the Internet listserv *H-Asia* discussed the question of how to teach the Asian survey course, an introductory course that often meets students' diversification or general education requirements and that may be their only course about Asia, while serving at the same time as an entree to other courses or even a major in Asian studies. Teaching a survey of Asia, as "fantastically diversified" as that area may be, is surely no more difficult than teaching analogous survey courses such as Western Civilization or World History. Developing an effective survey course of any stripe is a challenge to which there is no easy solution. Finding a comfortable balance between generalizations and large trends on the one hand, and enough specificity and detail on the other, is something each survey course teacher has to do for himself or herself. At the very least, however, the introductory survey of Asia these days should make students aware of the very artificiality of the construct "Asia." If, despairing of making all the pieces of Asia fit, a teacher concentrates on only one or two regions in the survey course (generally East Asia and Northeast Asia), it would be best to aim for truth in advertising, labeling such courses as surveys of the regions they actually do cover, rather than reproducing the common misconception that Asia *really* means China and Japan.

My goal in any introductory course, whether in my discipline of anthropology or in Asian studies, is to motivate students to learn more about the subject than they can possibly cover in the course. In the case of an Asian studies introductory course, we can imagine a number of desirable outcomes for our students. Some will continue their study of Asia through additional classes; some will not, but can still exit our classroom and their undergraduate careers with a lifelong interest in

Asia that they will pursue informally. Of several challenges that are familiar to the introductory survey teacher—to teach a course that is comprehensive, challenging, memorable, coherent, and interesting—the last two are by far the most important. One can neither adequately "cover the territory" nor ensure that the many facts that students encounter in the course will stick very long past the final exam, but if the readings are interesting and the classroom atmosphere is serious, exciting, and challenging, students will want to learn more after the term is over.

Having moved increasingly into active learning pedagogy over the last several years, I have learned to resist the urge to get through at all costs a predetermined list of topics that introductory texts in my discipline imply are essential.[54] Lectures have given way to structured, small-group discussions or problem solving, enactments, debates, in-class writing assignments—any variety of things I can think of to keep students actively constructing and stating the knowledge for themselves rather than merely trying to absorb it from me. As one friend in education expressed it, be "not the sage on the stage, but the guide on the side."[55] While the span of the materials I cover in my courses has shrunk, there are compensating gains in the extent to which students master and understand what we do cover. Above all, the classroom experience holds their interest and attention, and, I hope, hooks them on the materials and questions.

Since coherence also enhances the extent to which students find class materials interesting, survey courses organized around a theme or comparative thread are often more valuable than those which aim merely to cover a territory or a period. The theme could be anything from a world systems framework to specific social-historical topics such as gender and sexuality. Focusing on a theme bypasses much significant information, of course, but the grounds of selection are at least transparent. Instead of aiming to distill the whole, the goal is only to present students with an intellectual appetizer for a feast they must continue to seek in other places.

Remapping the Classroom

In a *Peanuts* cartoon, Lucy is watching television when Linus peeks over the side of her armchair and says proudly, "Guess what I learned in school today. We were having lunch and I learned how to open a bag of potato chips." Lucy, still looking at the television, queries, "What's the capital of Norway?" Deflated now, Linus responds, "Who knows?"

The study of geography fell out of fashion decades ago. "Most college-aged Americans," Lewis and Wigen observe, "have never explicitly studied geography, since most primary and secondary schools discontinued teaching the subject in the 1960s on the theory that memorization would stultify young minds."[56] While this is changing back again at the elementary and high school levels, the situation remains "grim" in higher education, where many geography programs were closed, and their faculty dispersed to other departments.[57] Geography remains a marginalized discipline on many campuses, if it has a presence at all. It is ironic that, although everyone talks about globalization, most students have only the vaguest sense of the world's geopolitics, and that, even as environmental activism is popular among students, colleges and universities may not provide a place to learn about environmental constraints, the diverse uses of space around the world, and the sometimes profound implications of these for human life.

Geography across the curriculum is one obvious response to this situation, although this does not substitute fully for a place in the curriculum where expert attention can be focused explicitly on issues of space and the environment. Still, some attention to these issues can often enliven and deepen courses directed to other ends. *Education About Asia* frequently contains articles with a geographic component and once devoted a special issue to the topic.[58] History, languages, religion, art history—almost everything we teach provides the opportunity to introduce maps and to consider how space and the environment have impacted the subject at hand. I have taught a course called Cultures of Southeast Asia in a number of different ways—organized around the rise of the state and how states work in this region, or, lately, organized through reading literature such as novels, memoirs, and short stories. Regardless of the course structure, maps are an essential aid, whether I provide handouts for the class, utilize a slide of a map, find something on the Internet to project from the computer, or resort to the standard rack of rolled maps at the front of the room. Making a game or a group competition of a map quiz or devising group problem solving with maps introduces variety to the usual lecture and discussion routine. My students, who readily admit how clueless they are about geography, often approach these tasks with great interest and concentration, as if grateful to have the excuse to spend this time with maps.

Most recently, I organized the Cultures of Southeast Asia course around the theme of nationalism. The first third of the course, subtitled "Traditional Neverlands," explored through memoirs the myth of a changeless traditional world before a nationalist "awakening." Novels about that awakening took up the middle of the course, which ended with a section called "Reality Shocks: After the Revolution." Novels set in Singapore and Vietnam explored postindependence difficulties and disillusionments.[59] After we had read the Philippine novel *Dusk*, by F. Sionil José, I gave breakout groups an enlarged copy of a relief map of Luzon and a list of some thirty place names, including rivers and mountains, to find on the map.[60] The work sheet included space to discuss and note briefly how and when each place was mentioned in the narrative. Set during the revolutions against the Spanish and the Americans, *Dusk* relates one man's dawning sense of nationalism, a process that José metaphorizes as a journey. The story is constructed, in fact, around two long and arduous travels by foot and horseback, and visualizing these routes on the map was essential to students' understanding it.

Recalling the arguments that began this chapter, however, we know that remapping the classroom does not mean merely a return to the study of geography as we learned it, if, indeed, we were lucky enough to have learned it. Every use of a map is also an opportunity to draw critical attention to the map itself as an artifact and to the constructedness of phenomena such as continents, regions, boundaries, and states. Where and when was this map made, and whose perspective does it portray? We will need to remind students that maps are always a *selective depiction* reflecting the questions and interests of the map maker, and, speaking historically, "that maps are, in essence, the very symbols of possession and instruments of plunder."[61]

Conclusion

We have reason for optimism about the future of Asian studies in liberal arts colleges. Acknowledging the constructedness of area designations such as Asia and its subregions, we can help our students understand what it means to map the earth in various ways. Listening carefully to their discourse about culture in the classroom, we can teach against usages implying that ideas and ways of behaving inhere in persons. We can make them more conscious of the way races, as socially constructed categories, have shaped Asian history as well as contemporary identity struggles. Above all, we can equip them to critique culturalist explanations that employ terms such as "culture" or "civilization" as overly powerful explanatory tools, homogenizing cultures and societies in the process, and imputing to them an essential changelessness. Understanding how power influences the ascendency of certain ideas and practices over competing others, and recognizing the heterogeneity of experiences within any Asian society, students gain in the process a more critical appreciation of how power and difference shape their own lives, not just those in distant times and places.

This restates the goal of teaching about Asia as a part of humane literacy. We should teach against everyday ways of speaking of culture and Asia, not just to be current with the latest academic trends, but to encourage in our students a certain *kind* of humane literacy that equips them for what lies ahead: continual change in their own and others' lives, the continuing expansion of information and its accelerating rate of exchange, a world increasingly one in terms of its shrinking size and also in its environmental and social challenges. Globalization does not mean, however, that English will get our students everywhere they might want to go, and it does not mean that the rest of the world is becoming just like us.[62] It does mean that we have to be all the more careful in negotiating and understanding difference. Speaking a person's primary language will remain a key to establishing trust and understanding, and language—written or spoken—will remain our surest and deepest access to other worlds to live in. Language study, combined with courses in history, the arts, religion, sociology, political science, and so on, is still the best road to understanding Asian lives, a long road for which there is no shortcut. Fortunately, there is hardly a road more scenic.

As Asianists increasingly find positions in liberal arts colleges, perhaps struggling to remap the ambitions they embraced in graduate school, they will see that these very special and almost uniquely American institutions are congenial to those who can embrace the challenges and freedoms of wearing many hats—teaching, building a disciplinary identity, and exercising commitment to the study of Asia. In fact, "Asian studies plus," that is, an area expertise that informs and is informed by disciplinary conversations, is perhaps easier to achieve here than in most other kinds of educational environments, both because Asian studies is less "centered," and also because in these teaching-focused settings, the disciplines, too, are less materially formidable.

In an essay forecasting the role of the humanities in the next century, Pauline Yu, Dean of the Humanities at the University of California, Los Angeles, cites extensively from Bill Readings' *The University in Ruins.* Yu's vision of how the academy *should* work, with scholars moving fluidly among different intellectual vantages, is how it does work, at least some of the time, for many of us at liberal arts colleges who participate not only in our departmental life, but also in multiple interdisciplinary programs. Critical and radical rethinking of area studies can be one product of this going back and forth, but so can a commensurate rethinking of disciplinary assumptions. Yu wrote the following:

> Readings proposes the adoption of "a certain rhythm of disciplinary attachment and detachment": intentionally impermanent collaborations that resist institutional entrenchment and inertia. And rather than involving an exchange of "the rigid and outmoded disciplines for a simply amorphous disciplinary space," this loosening of structures ought to provide an opportunity to foreground disciplinarity itself "as a *permanent question.* The short-term projects [he suggests] are designed to keep open the question of what it means to group knowledges in certain ways, and what it has meant that they have been so grouped in the past."[63]

While this remains only an ideal throughout the academy, it seems attainable, if anywhere, in small, liberal arts institutions.

Notes

1. Edward W. Said, *Orientalism.*
2. Partha Chatterjee, *Nationalist Thought and the Colonial World,* 60.
3. David Landes, *The Wealth and Poverty of Nations,* 213–30.
4. Andre Gunder Frank, *ReOrient,* 111–17; see also Felipe Fernández-Armesto, *Millennium,* 13.
5. Jack Goody, *The East in the West,* 7.
6. Eric R. Wolf, *Europe and the People Without History,* 18.
7. Clifford critiques Said's *Orientalism,* and other postmodern writing, on precisely this point. James Clifford, *The Predicament of Culture,* 272.
8. Martin W. Lewis and Kären E. Wigen, *The Myth of Continents,* 10, 194. The authors term this "cartographic ethnocentrism." An imagined Thai version of this phenomenon occurs in a scene in the movie *The King and I* (1956) in which the British governess disabuses the royal children of the assumption that Siam is the center of the world and that it dwarfs its nearest neighbors. She replaces their ill-proportioned map with another representing the "truth" of modern cartography.
9. Lewis and Wigen, *The Myth of Continents,* 16.
10. Ibid., 37.
11. Ibid., 166–69; Terrill E. Lautz, "Financing Contemporary China Studies," 305.
12. For a critique of these categories, see Ravi Arvind Palat, "Fragmented Visions," 279.
13. Lewis and Wigen, *The Myth of Continents,* 211–12 (n. 22).
14. Benedict R. O'G. Anderson, *Imagined Communities.*
15. Lewis and Wigen, *The Myth of Continents,* 8.

16. Thongchai Winichakul, *Siam Mapped*, 17.

17. Prasenjit Duara, *Rescuing History from the Nation*; Gail Hershatter, Emily Honig, Jonathan N. Lipman, and Randall Stross, ed., *Remapping China*, 5–7; K.W. Taylor, "Surface Orientations in Vietnam," 973.

18. Katherine Bowie, *Rituals of National Loyalty*; Sheldon Garon, *Molding Japanese Minds*.

19. Lewis and Wigen, *The Myth of Continents*, 173. Whether Southeast Asia exhibits a cultural and historical unity or is largely a residue of what is left over after carving up other such regions is a contested issue. Anthony Reid, *Southeast Asia in the Age of Commerce, 1450–1680*, vol. 1, 6, makes the case for Southeast Asia's cultural coherence.

20. Lewis and Wigen, *The Myth of Continents*, 186.

21. Ibid., 192.

22. Tu Wei-ming, "Cultural China: The Periphery as the Center," 13. See also Matthew Ciolek's essay titled "Asian Studies and the WWW," in which he says, "more information *about* Asia seems to come from regions situated outside the continent than within it" (Web site *http://www.ciolek.com/PAPERS/pnc-taipei-98.html*).

23. Lila Abu-Lughod, "Writing Against Culture"; Christoph Brumann, "Writing for Culture."

24. Verena Stolcke, "Talking Culture," 2.

25. Ibid., 4. For another comparison with discourse about race, see Joel Kahn, "Culture," 17–21.

26. Ann Laura Stoler, "Rethinking Colonial Categories," 135–38; Nicholas Thomas, *Colonialism's Culture*, 14; Frances Gouda, *Dutch Culture Overseas*, 118–57.

27. Two Southeast Asian novels about nationalist consciousness that illustrate this are F. Sionil José's *Dusk, a Novel*, about the Philippines; and *This Earth of Mankind* by Pramoedya Ananta Toer, about Indonesia.

28. Jacquie Miller and Jonathon Gatehouse, "Rainbow Families," *Gazette*.

29. George W. Stocking, Jr., *Race, Culture, and Evolution*, 231.

30. Kamala Visweswaran, "Race and the Culture of Anthropology," 70–73.

31. Clifford Geertz, "From the Native's Point of View."

32. Robert Borofsky, *Making History*, 186.

33. Lars Rodseth, "Distributive Models of Culture," 57.

34. Brumann, "Writing for Culture," S6–S7.

35. Roger Keesing, "Theories of Culture Revisited," 309.

36. Neil Jamieson, *Understanding Vietnam*, 15–41. Jamieson's solution organizes the diversity of Vietnamese culture and history around the familiar yin/yang polarity, a device that some critics denounce; see, for example, David Marr's review of *Understanding Vietnam*, 1005–07. For contradictions between patrilineal descent and a bilateral kinship terminology, see Hy Van Luong, " 'Brother' and 'Uncle.' "

37. James L. Watson, ed., *Golden Arches East*.

38. Jack Goody, *The East in the West*, 235. See also Robert W. Hefner, ed., *Market Cultures*, 3–4.

39. Samuel P. Huntington, *The Clash of Civilizations and the Remaking of World Order*.

40. Ibid., 29.

41. Robert W. Hefner, ed., *Market Cultures*, 29.

42. Robert W. Hefner, ed., *Democratic Civility*, 20.

43. Marshall Sahlins, *Islands of History*, ix–x.

44. Charles Hockett, *The State of the Art*, 82–85.

45. In the same period, some granting agencies—the Carnegie Corporation, American Council of Learned Societies, the Ford Foundation, and the Rockefeller Foundation—funded a number of faculty and curricular development projects in a handful of liberal arts colleges. See Ward Morehouse, ed., *Asian Studies in Liberal Arts Colleges*, 13, 32, 43.

46. Stanley O'Connor, "Humane Literacy and Southeast Asian Art," 147.

47. Ibid., 156. This eloquent statement reminds us, too, that teachers at liberal arts colleges do not monopolize humanistic goals and a concern for teaching; O'Connor taught at Cornell, one of the preeminent research centers for the study of Southeast Asia.

48. International Liberal Arts Colleges, *In the International Interest*, "Executive Summary," II. See also Stephen Nussbaum, chapter four, in this volume.

49. International Liberal Arts Colleges, *In the International Interest*, "Executive Summary," III.

50. Palat, "Fragmented Visions," 286.

51. Anderson, *Imagined Communities*; James C. Scott, *The Moral Economy of the Peasant*; James C. Scott, Weapons of the Weak; Clifford Geertz, *The Interpretation of Cultures*.

52. Palat, "Fragmented Visions," 288.

53. Carlos Bulosan, *America Is in the Heart*; Stephen Griffiths, *Emigrants, Entrepreneurs, and Evil Spirits*.

54. The two pedagogical books most useful to me have been Chet Meyers and Thomas B. Jones, *Promoting Active Learning*; and Charles C. Bonwell and James A. Eison, *Active Learning*.

55. I thank Nancy J. Keiser, chair of the Division of Education at Mount St. Clare College, for introduction to this pithy aphorism. She participated with me in the ASIANetwork Ford Foundation Faculty Curricular Development Seminar on Southeast Asia in 1998 and 1999.

56. Lewis and Wigen, *Myth of Continents*, xii.

57. See Geography Education Standards Project, *Geography for Life*, for an outline of what students should know at different K–12 levels.

58. The *Education About Asia* special issue on geography is vol. 3, no. 1 (Spring 1998). See also vol. 3, no. 2, for an article about teaching geography using the city (Bangkok), and vol. 3, no. 3, for an article about South Asian cities and another about teaching Indonesia from a world systems perspective.

59. I used Duong Thu Huong's *Paradise of the Blind*, set in postrevolutionary Vietnam, and Philip Jeyaretnam's *Abraham's Promise*, a novel set in contemporary Singapore.

60. José, *Dusk*.

61. Palat, "Fragmented Visions," 281. See also Matthew Edney, *Mapping an Empire*, 1–2; and James C. Scott, *Seeing Like a State*, 44–47.

62. In an essay on the past and future of Asian Studies on the World Wide Web, T. Matthew Ciolek noted the growth of a number of different language communities on the Web. According to Ciolek, while English predominates as the language for "external consumption," vernaculars continue to be used for much internal dialog and communication (Web site *http://www.ciolek.com/PAPERS/pnc-taipei-98.html*).

63. Pauline Yu, "The Course of the Particulars," 28. Citations from Bill Readings, *The University in Ruins*, 176–77.

6

Where We Came From, Where We Are Going

Ainslie T. Embree

"Now that the sage-kings are no more," Xunzi, the Chinese philosopher, wrote sometime in the third century B.C.E., "the preserving of names has become lax, strange terminology has arisen, and names and their actualities have become confused."[1] As they teach others, he sensibly argued, scholars to avoid confusion should make clear what old names they are retaining, while sometimes giving new meanings to them, and what new ones they are creating, often, some of us may feel, using strange terminology. This chapter is an attempt, however oblique, to clarify Asian studies in the context of the actualities of American liberal arts colleges and liberal education. Its immodest aim is to suggest that while Asian studies programs became part of the undergraduate curriculum somewhat by the back door, they have gained a commanding place in liberal education. A discussion of where we came from is intertwined with one on where we are going, for in the academic world, more perhaps than elsewhere, the future is hostage to the past.

Our liberal arts colleges are peculiarly American institutions, however nostalgically we may seek their roots in Oxford, Paris, or Padua. A useful survey has identified 212 of them, which, while enormously diverse, share characteristics that lead the author to conclude that "no other country has schools committed so clearly to the highest quality of undergraduate education." This large claim is based on what they share in common: they are largely residential and relatively small; they attempt to be comprehensive in terms of the humanities, social sciences, and sciences; they emphasize student-teacher interaction; and they are primarily committed to undergraduate education.[2] Another well-known study, made at the end of World War II by the Harvard College faculty, defines the purpose of such liberal arts colleges as helping students realize the "unique, particular functions in life which is in them to fulfill," and to prepare them for those "common spheres which as citizens and heirs of a joint culture, they share with others."[3] At the end of World War I, the faculty of the undergraduate college at Columbia University, as they prepared to educate a new generation, concluded that all students should have a core education in the history and literature of the culture and civilization of which they were the heirs. Liberal arts colleges in the United States have never aspired to be ivory towers, and these reports, like many of the others that were produced, insisted that the justification for the colleges was the preparation of leaders and citizens who could respond to the changing needs of a free and democratic society.

At the end of the twentieth century, an urgent question forced itself on our attention: What is this common culture and civilization to which these reports refer and in which all students share? It was assumed in almost all liberal arts colleges that the common culture for all students, at the heart of the core curriculum, would be the history and culture of the Western world, meaning essentially Western Europe and North America, with its origins in Greece and Rome. It is this assumption that was challenged in the liberal arts colleges, at first rather timidly and almost with apologies, after the end of World War II, by Asian studies.

Where We Came From

The phrase "Asian studies" itself is a source of confusion, needing clarification, for it is a new introduction into American academic discourse. "Asia" is, of course, an ancient word, coming to us from the Greeks, to whom it meant Anatolia, Persia, and the Indian subcontinent. Eventually the increase of geographic knowledge added China, Japan, and Southeast Asia, but Asia was never thought of by serious writers as having social or political unity. Many of the famous Enlightenment figures, including Voltaire and Montesquieu, drew interesting comparisons between China and Europe, usually to China's advantage, but what is generally regarded as the beginning of scholarly interest in Asia, at least in the English-speaking world, was the founding of the Asiatic Society in Bengal in 1784 by Sir William Jones, the famous philologist. It was the first of many such societies, with the purpose, according to Sir William, of "inquiring into the history, civil and natural, the antiquities, arts, sciences, and literature, of Asia."[4] This could serve as a description in a college catalog for what we now call Asian studies. These early Orientalists, as they were called, assumed, as self-evident, that their motivation was personal curiosity, but that this knowledge of Asia would be interesting to all educated people. They also assumed that it would be valuable to Europeans as they became rulers of large Asian territories. In our own time, however, the motivation of Westerners in engaging in Asian studies, has been given a more sinister interpretation.

Edward Said, a literary critic who was deeply involved in the Palestinian movement, has given an immensely influential interpretation of Western motivation in studying other cultures in his book *Orientalism*.[5] While he is careful to note that his criticism is mainly concerned with treatment of the Middle East in both scholarly and popular literature, other scholars have extended his arguments to writing on the rest of Asia.[6] Orientalism, his word for what he regards as a pervasive attitude in the West, is, he argues, a mode of discourse by which the West created an image of the Islamic Middle East as the Orient in order to control it. The academic community was linked with a network of corporate business, foundations, oil companies, missionary societies, the military, the foreign service, and the intelligence community in order to preserve Western dominance through the manipulation of knowledge.[7] James Clifford, a thoughtful critic of Said's work, while accepting many of his insights, suggests that the motivation for the study of other cultures may more certainly be rooted in what Said himself calls "a generalized condition of homelessness," a sense of dissatisfaction with answers given within one's own culture.[8] This seems a realistic reading of the interest of many undergraduates in Asian studies, but there has been a marked change in recent years. More students are being motivated by finding, as a well-informed observer has put it, especially in studying about China, "an image of Asia that is dynamic, fluid, and full of present-tense challenges and opportunities."[9]

The presence of Asian studies on American campuses is generally credited to the changed political and social conditions after the end of World War II, and this is correct, particularly for graduate studies, but they have a longer lineage that has special relevance for liberal education. In 1783, a year before the Asiatic Society was founded in Bengal, Ezra Stiles, the President of Yale College, made what is perhaps the first reference in the United States to the importance of Asian studies for the new nation that was being born.[10] Whether this had anything to do with the fact that the college was named after a benefactor who had made his money in India is not certain, but Stiles asserted that the prosperity and splendor of the United States would be built in part upon a relationship with Asia. The new American flag would soon fly around the globe, displaying "the thirteen stripes and the new constellation at Bengal and Canton, on the Indus and the Ganges, on the Whang-ho and the Yangste-Kiang." The ships would bring back more than material goods, however: they would import into America "the wisdom and literature of the east." Having been brought to these shores, the knowledge and learning of India and China would be here "digested and carried to its highest perfection." Then comes Stiles's great vision of what would happen to the learning of the East in America. Having been brought to this country, it would be refined and transformed and would "reblaze back from America to Europe, Asia, and Africa and illumine the world with truth and liberty."[11]

It is pleasant to think that Asian studies in American liberal arts colleges is a direct product of this grand vision, but it was slow of fulfillment and there were many divergent streams that led to the present. American scholars have contributed insights and new understanding to the classical learning of all the great Asian traditions, and their views have won acceptance and praise from their peers in China, India, and Japan, moving beyond translations of the great seminal works to interpretations of their meaning and relevance for the present day. Thus, for example, in arguments that have been accepted by Chinese scholars, American scholars have demonstrated that Confucian thought locates human rights as authentic to the mainstream of Chinese civilization, and not, as sometimes argued, a Western imposition.[12] A point also worth noting and emphasizing is that many of the foremost of younger American scholars in Asian studies, although it would be invidious to name them, found the focus for their academic careers in courses on Asia in liberal arts colleges.

Scholarly study of aspects of Asian history and culture had begun in a tentative way, and in 1842 the American Oriental Society was organized. The interests of its members were mainly philological, especially in studies of ancient Egypt and Mesopotamia that related to biblical history, and later to Islamic and Sanskrit studies, and much less to Chinese and Japanese studies, and always with an emphasis on the premodern.

Between the two world wars, there was increased interest in Asia in the United States, and organizations were formed to educate the general public and policy makers about the need to take seriously events in Asia, especially in China and Japan, that would affect American foreign policy. The best known of these was the Institute of Pacific Relations, an international organization with an important American branch founded in 1925. After World War II, especially in the McCarthy era, some of its members were accused, rightly or wrongly, of being pro-communist. What is undoubtedly true is that it represented a tendency among scholars and others interested in Asia to be passionate advocates for specific American policies toward different Asian countries, especially China.

The first academic organization wholly devoted to Asian studies was the Far Eastern Association, founded in 1941, which defined its area of interest not as Asia but as China, Japan, Southeast Asia, and Northeast Asia, another reminder that scholars rarely thought in terms of Asia, but rather in terms of its regions. Asia did not appear in the name of an academic organization until 1956, when the membership of the Far Eastern Association voted to include South Asia as one of its regions of concern, changing their name to the Association for Asian Studies. South Asia was the term coined—largely by the American Department of State—to replace India, which had been the name in the West for the region since ancient times, but with the creation of Pakistan a more inclusive designation was needed. As the historian of the new association notes with some delicacy, the members of the old association "did not welcome South Asia into its realm of responsibility without misgivings."[13] Some East Asian specialists objected on the grounds that the title implied a common civilization throughout Asia; others objected that the South Asianists were carpetbaggers, seeking to move in on better established fields. Still others, however, felt the association would be strengthened by new members and that the foundations, especially Ford, would be impressed and willing to give money if the scholars showed a desire to create a larger body of area studies.

While many members of the Association for Asian Studies (AAS) were teachers in liberal arts colleges, scholars from the graduate programs in the larger universities dominated it in its early years. A simple statistic is significant for the growth of Asian studies at liberal arts college. While in the early years the leadership was drawn from the large eastern universities, in 1999, of the 40 positions of leadership in the AAS, not a single one was drawn from them, with 12 coming from small liberal arts colleges.[14] There is little reference to Asian studies at the undergraduate level in the association's early years, but in fact leadership for its introduction came from two large research universities, Columbia and Chicago, both of which had small liberal arts colleges that were proud of their distinctive under-graduate teaching. Conferences held under their auspices from 1957 to 1960 are the beginning of the movement to establish undergraduate Asian studies, and the reports that came out of them tell, in a quite striking fashion, where we came from and where we are going. Reading the names of those who attended and took positions of leadership, and the positions they advanced, one is reminded of Xunzi's sage kings and the changes that have followed their departure.

Two of the earliest conferences, held in Chicago, did not concern themselves with Asian studies as such, but only with India and China. The published reports suggest that the problem the participants were wrestling with was bringing the study of the various great Asian civilizations from the specializations of the graduate schools, where they were just beginning to make an impact, into the wider world of undergraduate education. One report of a conference in 1957 was titled *Introducing India in Liberal Education* and the other, in the next year, was *Chinese Civilization in Liberal Education*.[15] The introduction to the volume on India stated the purpose of the conference in a fashion that probably would have been accepted by all the participants, if such unlikely unanimity can be assumed among a group of senior academics:

> (1) To communicate a solid understanding of a long-established and well-developed non-Western civilization and of a critically important area in the contemporary world, and (2) To provide students with a different kind of educational experience which by portraying a contrasted great civilization will sharpen and deepen their understanding of their own culture.[16]

From the perspective of forty years later, the first statement seems to be identifying and privileging "high" civilizations, and the second appears to be accepting that the students have a common culture as their intellectual legacy. In the context of the time, however, these statements were a challenge to what was still a Eurocentric point of view, as it was when a generation earlier a critic could accuse the leaders of higher education of wanting to make the United States "nothing more than a spiritual colony of Europe, dependent upon the mother continent for all the meanings that dignify man and ennoble his works."[17] In urging the value of studying about Indian and Chinese civilizations, scholars were furthering, perhaps unwittingly, the educational philosophy of John Dewey who, long before at Chicago, had said that education was one of the great opportunities for pioneering. From changes in the curriculum would come "versatility and inventiveness, ready adaptation to new conditions, minds of courage and fertility in facing obstacles."[18]

Conferences at Columbia University in 1958 and 1961 championed comprehensive undergraduate courses that would be introductions to at least four of the historic civilizations of Asia. The report on the conference on the humanities, called *Approaches to Oriental Classics*, included, in addition to discussions of works from the Indian, Chinese, and Japanese traditions, consideration of literature from the Islamic traditions of Asia.[19] In a second edition thirty years later of a few of the original essays but with new additions, William Theodore de Bary, the driving force at Columbia and elsewhere for courses of this kind, noted a radical change that had taken place in the use of the term "classics" since the first conference was held. The terms "classics" and "canon" were used in 1959 without self-consciousness, because it was assumed that in the multicultural world there were a plurality of canons. By the 1990s, however, we faced, he noted, "nothing less than a radical, cultural-revolutionary challenge to any kind of canon, Eastern or Western."[20] He leaves the question of canons without much argument, perhaps like Churchill, believing that if we open a quarrel between the past and present, we shall find that we have lost the future. The second conference, in 1961, was concerned with teaching about Asian civilizations. There were contributions by eminent scholars in various disciplines dealing with Asia, but, the preface insists, there were no "area" specialists present, a reminder that by then the term had been rejected by many scholars concerned with aspects of civilization and culture. Why, then, have courses labeled Asian civilizations? Summarizing the arguments, de Bary suggested that while studying the various Asian civilizations in one course was obviously a daunting undertaking for teacher and student, it provides an opportunity to compare, not the West with Asia, but India and China and Japan with each other.[21]

The optimism, common sense, and wisdom shown by the advocates of Asian studies in the undergraduate curriculum did not, of course, go unchallenged. The general argument used against the new development, then as now, was that undergraduates should be grounded in their own culture before being exposed to alien ones. A memorable—ill-natured and ill-informed, but widely publicized—attack came forty years after the pioneer Chicago and Columbia conferences from Allan Bloom, a professor of classics at Chicago. "Sexual adventurers like Margaret Mead," he announced, were urging us to go to "the bazaar of cultures" and "told us that not only must we know other cultures and learn to respect them, but we could also learn from them."[22] That was, in fact, what the scholars in Asian studies were doing, but from a different perspective. The importance of Bloom's strange tirade is, unfortunately, that its substance still has wide currency.

These academic discourses on Asian studies in liberal arts education were taking place at a time in the history of higher education that have been succinctly labeled, in Robert McCaughey's erudite and witty history of international education in the United States, as "The Years That Were Fat."[23] This phrasing is apt because of perceived national needs after World War II as the United States undertook the enormous responsibilities of being a world power. In 1948, according to John Gardner, then president of the Carnegie Corporation, while ordinary citizens needed knowledge of the world, as did college-age students, the most pressing need was to increase the number of what he described as "that pitifully small corps of experts on each of the various areas of the world."[24] It was to train such experts that not only the great foundations, such as Ford, Carnegie, and Rockefeller, but many smaller ones, poured vast sums into graduate programs for international studies at the major universities. Significantly, the U.S. government through the National Defense Education Act of 1959 provided for the training in the languages and cultures of areas that had been little studied before. This included, of course, all the major regions of Asia, above all China and Japan, one a former friend in the process of becoming an enemy, the other a former enemy in the process of becoming a friend. To a much lesser extent, attention was given to South Asia and Southeast Asia, areas that had received minimal attention in any American university before 1950, perhaps because they were neither friends nor enemies, but former possessions of European imperial powers.

The term "area studies" is an example of what Xunzi meant by strange terminology that causes confusion. It is a term little used by specialists in studies of Asia, and it refers far more to studies at the graduate level than to undergraduate Asian studies. It was a designation used by administrators and funding agencies as a convenient label for the new kinds of studies that were organized to meet national and academic needs, perhaps best exemplified in the Ford Foundation's Foreign Area Fellowship Program. To encourage broad competence, students who were funded under the program were required, in addition to courses in their discipline, to do intensive language study and to take a variety of courses on their area in other disciplines.

While the funds that subsidized area studies were welcomed by university administrators and by specialists in the various areas, there was always considerable opposition to the new developments from those who felt that disciplinary rigor was being sacrificed. Robert Bates, a Harvard political scientist, for example, questioned the legitimacy of area specialists in his own discipline, because, he argued, they were more interested in the languages and cultures of their area than with comparisons with political institutions elsewhere.[25] This was not a charge that scholars studying Chinese history or Indian political science could easily deny, even if they wanted to. Historians in the established fields of American and European history were probably envious of the largess that seemed to pass them by, leaving them without a second historian on Reconstruction, while a historian was appointed to teach Southeast Asian history. Economists soon opted out, on the grounds that area specialists were not needed for the problems that interested them; knowledge of Javanese literature was not useful in managing the Indonesia economy.

One must be brutally frank at this point: much of the opposition to so-called area studies comes from scholars who begrudge any expenditure of funds on areas outside the United States and Europe. This led Dean Lisa Anderson of Columbia University—which has what is probably the largest number of area studies centers in the country—to remark, rather ruefully, "People recognize that we are one of the last bastions of area studies, so there is a live-and-let-live attitude."[26] In passing it may be noted that those area studies centers at Columbia had little direct connection with the flourishing undergraduate Asian program at the university and, indeed, they sometimes actively opposed it. This was not an uncommon pattern elsewhere.

Graduate schools see their proper function as training students in particular disciplines to produce specialists. Abraham Flexner, one of the great proponents of research universities, was convinced, according to one account, that universities are for the pursuit of new knowledge, and they should not be deflected from this purpose by the transmission to undergraduates of knowledge that has already been accumulated.[27] Asian studies programs in the liberal arts colleges, it is true, do not have as their primary concern the producing of experts in some discipline related to Asia, but many of the students who have participated in them are among our best research scholars. They gained from programs that aimed at a liberal education, not training for a career. The task of those who are proponents of Asian studies is, therefore, to demonstrate how it is integral to education at an American liberal arts college at this juncture of our history.

But, a sceptic may ask, "Why engage in liberal learning?" The best answer to that question, it has been suggested, is equally simple: "To learn something worth knowing for its own sake."[28] To a parent meeting the extortionate tuition demands of a private liberal arts college, that may sound unconvincing and precious, but in truth it encapsulates what a liberal education tries to accomplish. This is so because "something worth knowing" carries meanings that are central to liberal education. The acquisition of information is, of course, important, but not just any stray pieces of information, rather, material that can add meaning and richness to life. This is, or should be, at the forefront of the thinking of every curriculum committee. In his book *The Disciplined Mind: What All Students Should Understand*, Howard Gardner argues that students must acquire facts, not simply as information, but as part of "probing important issues and learning how to think about them in disciplined ways." He goes on to say, "In the absence of disciplinary ways of thinking, cultural literacy lacks an epistemological home; it amounts to a hodgepodge of concepts and facts."[29]

Most of us who have taught courses in Asian studies to undergraduates would argue that confrontation with new ideas forces students to think coherently about the meaning of different patterns of thought and different answers to life's perplexing problems. That courses in Asian studies programs can do this is what makes them at once so exciting and so dangerous. It was the danger of new ways of looking at the world that the members of the school board of Lake County in Florida had in mind when they objected to the mandate of the state that there should be teaching about other cultures in the schools. They agreed to do so, under financial pressure, but with the proviso that the teachers would stress that American family values and other basic values "are superior to other foreign or historic cultures."[30] Such objections to teaching Asian studies are probably not likely to arise in liberal arts colleges, but surely one result will be some questioning of the assumptions by which we live. Asian studies should do something analogous to what an art critic argues that contemporary art does through a continuous stressing of the value of discovery. What a teacher or critic can do, he said, is "to sort out those aging ideas that get encrusted around past creative achievements and clog the proper working of the imagination in changing times."[31]

Where We Are Going

It is precisely through the working of the imagination that Asian studies can become integrated into the academic life of the liberal arts college. This can be done through involvement, sometimes in resistance, sometimes in collaboration, with issues and trends in the general intellectual life of our changing times. Radical curricular changes are not needed to relate Asian studies to such concerns, but recognition of their value to a common cause of living a good life in a good society. This is not a one-way street of teachers preparing students for their lives after college, but of both being engaged in a common enterprise in exploring the range of human possibility in the ambiguities and contradictions of the world we inhabit.

As the chapters in this volume have indicated, the varieties of Asian studies in our colleges are products of both individual preferences and institutional structures, and ideal models need to be molded to fit practical realities. This is especially true as we turn from looking at the question "Where did we come from?" to "Where are we going?" The answer to the second question, while it is largely determined by where we have been, must also take into account issues that are part of contemporary discourse in the academic world that are shaping the intellectual context in which Asian studies must find their place.

Three sets of such issues occupy some of the same intellectual territory that Asian studies does in the curriculum, intersecting with each other in terms of cooperation and competition. The three are multiculturalism, ethnic studies, and world history. The merits and meaning of all three have been debated in both academic and public settings, very often stridently and with a lack of mutual understanding. The debate, however, is a necessary part of the dialog that goes on between cultures and between the past and the present, which is another definition of liberal education. The future of undergraduate Asian studies programs will be determined in large part by our meaningful participation in that dialog.

Multiculturalism, which has been a battle cry for opposing factions in American educational discourse, must be seen in the context of liberal democracy's acceptance of both the value and the inevitability of diversity in personal and political life. Understood in this social context, multiculturalism, in the words of a thoughtful critic, "enriches our world by exposing us to different cultural and intellectual perspectives, and thereby increasing our possibilities for intellectual and spiritual growth, exploration, and enlightenment."[32] While this statement marches closely with rationales put forward in the chapters in this book, some critics have seen it simply as a restatement of the Orientalism excoriated by Said and others. If critics from the right denounce liberal pluralists for downgrading the Western tradition, those from the left, as Henry Louis Gates, Jr., points out, criticize it for disguising the reality of power relationships by leaving hegemony intact as we make use of other cultures to improve our own lot. Pluralism "fails to be sufficiently emancipatory; it leaves oppressive structures intact."[33] Such arguments have been especially common in the writings of Indian scholars, who, perhaps sensitive to the continuing dominance of Western culture in Indian intellectual life, have denounced what they regard as the cultural imperialism of making use of data drawn from Indian experience in such disciplines as anthropology, literature, and religious studies.[34] The only answer one can make is that while the West has profited from its appropriation of knowledge and information of Asia, so have all cultures, not least those of Asia. We have been speaking of multiculturalism as an issue in American life, but it is of fundamental concern, in one form or another, in many of the cultural and national areas that are part of Asian studies programs. Charles Taylor has spoken of "the politics of recognition," by which he means the demand by groups for recognition of their distinctive identity and culture. Group identity is shaped positively by an awareness of cultural achievements, such as perceived literary, religious, or artistic greatness, and also negatively by misrecognition by others, so a group "can suffer real damage, real distortion, if the people or society around them mirror back to them a confining or demeaning or contemptible picture of themselves."[35]

To anyone familiar with the history of modern Asian states, the relevance of this analysis is clear. From China, at the beginning of the twenty-first century, the Tibetans and the Uighurs are case studies in how a government policy of permitting the existence of a multicultural pattern of society can be contradicted by group responses. The opening of schools and hospitals, the end of serfdom, the closing of what were regarded as parasitic monasteries, the building of highways, were for the Chinese the gifts of modernity, but for the Tibetans they were the destruction of their culture. The situation of the Uighurs has received less international publicity, but—stirred by restatements of Islam as a source of national identity—they have begun to resist the dilution of their area and their culture by Chinese government policies. Fifty years ago, a course on China in an undergraduate Asian studies program would almost certainly not have mentioned either of the groups; now a teacher who did not address the issue of multiculturalism and its meaning for China's historical experience would be missing an opportunity to deepen students' understanding of the forces creating the modern world. As for India, writers both Indian and foreign have exhausted language to describe its multicultural pluralism, which, the British rulers used to insist and many Indians still believe, made a democratic form of government impossible. Religious, linguistic, racial, and caste differences, coupled with the long experience of foreign invasions, demanded, according to John Morley, the British statesman at the beginning of the twentieth century who was responsible for instituting a small measure of self-government, the strong authoritarian rule the British had given. Without it, one would hear "through the dark distances the roar and scream of confusion and carnage in India."[36] In appeals to the past to explain the present, teachers must tread warily, with understanding based on knowledge. It is tempting and easy to explain, as newspaper accounts routinely do, the brutal conflicts in Kosovo and Kashmir by references to ancient hatreds and quarrels based on religion, when these are in fact being manufactured by politicians to inflame passions. The hard task, but one of the many values of an Asian studies program, is to examine how changing political, social, and economic structures can create conflict in a plural society when group identities assume new roles, and how religion can be used to legitimize violence.

A suggestive generalization on this theme from the writing of Jürgen Habermas can serve in an Asian studies program for explicating the relationships of past and present. In a modern democratic state, law protects the rights of individuals, but, he asks, "Can a theory of rights that is so individualistically constructed deal adequately with struggles for recognition in which it is the articulation and assertion of collective identities that seems to be at stake?"[37] Indian nationalism, for example, as institutionally articulated at the end of the nineteenth century in the Indian National Congress, had as its formal political philosophy ideas formulated by its leaders from the writings of nineteenth-century British liberal thinkers, such as John Stuart Mill. Perhaps even more important, if not so overtly stated, however, were ideas from the dominant Brahmanical culture of the Indian elites that composed its leadership.

What these two disparate streams had in common was not a denial of the existence of multiculturalism but a refusal to imagine a polity that would allow groups, and not just majorities composed of individuals, a constitutional role. The result was the emergence of an alternative nationalism, led by M.A. Jinnah, who identified the quarter of the Indian population who were adherents of Islam as a group with a collective identity. "Let me say again," he wrote Mahatma Gandhi in 1940, "India is not a nation, nor a country. It is a subcontinent of nationalities, Hindus and Muslims being the major nations."[38]

Whether the partition of India in 1947 was inevitable, given the nature of Indian society, whether it was due to the British or the Muslim leaders or the intransigence of Nehru and the Indian National Congress, the historical reality was two partitions. One in 1947 divided the British Empire in the Indian subcontinent into India and Pakistan. Then in 1971, the struggle for recognition on the part of the Bengali-speaking Muslims in East Pakistan led to the partition of the original Pakistan into a new Pakistan and Bangladesh. In studying this period, and many other similar situations, students and teachers have an opportunity to examine the perils of what Troy Duster, a careful American scholar of the social and political implications of multiculturalism, called a "binary conception" of cultural differences. The mistake is in supposing that societies have only two choices: "That different groups either shed their religious, philosophical and cultural differences, or there will be ethnic, racial, and religious enclaves with a perpetual danger of tribal war."[39] One can make a reasonable case for the proposition that Asian studies programs give new insights and guidance that lead to a deeper understanding of why such conflicts occur in multicultural societies and how they might be prevented.

Ethnic studies are often regarded as congruent with multiculturalism, but this can be misleading. The aspect of ethnic studies that will be noted here, that differentiates them from Asian studies, is the emphasis on serving specific groups defined by their ethnic self-identification within an academic setting. A broad distinction is that multiculturalism in the liberal arts college is advocated, as is Asian studies, for the total enrichment of the educational enterprise of the institution, and while ethnic studies should, of course, serve in the same way, in practice their focus locates them in a narrower range. Adding complexity to the discussion of such studies, is that ethnicity is used, particularly in political science, for the role of groups, defined by linguistic, religious, cultural, and historic inheritances, within the framework of a nation-state. In this sense, ethnicity will obviously be an important component of Asian studies, as noted above in the discussion of multiculturalism, whereas ethnic studies, as generally understood, will probably not be since they are basically concerned with groups resident in the United States. This is the point that is being made by Nathan Glazer when he claims that "We are all multiculturalists now."[40] He is arguing that changing patterns of migration, urbanism, and the recruitment of minority teachers and administrators have changed the kind of education given, at least in urban schools. Black studies as a field is a rejection of the old ideal of Americanization, of assimilation into the mainstream culture, and this has been because of a failure in the past to incorporate black Americans into the mainstream of civil society. This also perhaps explains why black Americans show, according to most anecdotal accounts, little interest in courses in Asian studies. They are too deeply engaged, to use K. Anthony Appiah's phrase, in seeking their own "identity, authenticity, and survival."[41]

While black studies, the original and most widespread variant of ethnic studies, born out of a singularly shameful history of oppression, may not seem to have much in common with Asian studies on our campuses, by its vigorous challenge to received patterns of education it has weakened assumptions about the privileged priority of the Western tradition. In doing so, black studies has almost certainly assured that the beachhead for the study of other cultures, first made by Asian studies, will not be seriously assaulted either from within or outside the academic world. Somewhat oddly, it is the vitality of black studies, not Asian studies, that led to the demand for Asian American studies, and, on many campuses, Asian American studies do not seem to have as close a relationship as might have been expected with Asian studies programs. "Asian" is somewhat of a misnomer, as most of the programs seem to be oriented toward East Asia, and only rarely to include a South Asian component.

There are a number of reasons for this lack of what might have been expected to be a symbiotic relationship between Asian American studies and Asian studies programs at liberal arts colleges. One is that the student protests of the 1960s and 1970s that led to a demand for black and Chicano studies were rooted in anger and frustration, reflected very often in the attitudes of faculty leaders of the movements. The same could rarely be said of faculty already engaged in teaching Asian studies or of the Asian American students on campuses across the country. They seem not to have been personally much burdened, as black students were, by a sense of being victims of oppression and discrimination either in the United States or in their countries of origin.

What did have some similarity to the black students' experience is what is often referred to, without much definition of its meaning, as a search for roots. For black Americans, this involved a search for identity and authenticity. For Asian Americans, it meant partly this, especially for students of Chinese origin, but less so for South Asians. Coming, on the whole, from a prosperous and well-educated community, often with well-defined religious orientation, South Asians helped to promote a course on Indian civilization that emphasized the wonder that was India in the ancient past and the harm done to a great civilization by invaders, first the Turks, identified by their religion, and then the British. Asian American studies, in contrast to Asian studies, was intended for a group that was Asian in origin, while the courses in Asian studies programs, though they of course welcomed students of all ethnic origins, were not meant to introduce students to their roots.

In insisting that Asian studies is not ethnic studies, as Asian American studies can rightly claim to be, a number of ancillary comments may be made. One is that in finding a location for Asian American studies in departmental structures, some colleges place it in the American studies program, but one well-known promoter of Asian American studies, Ronald Takaki of Berkeley, argues against this. He would locate it in a separate ethnic studies department, thereby contributing to the definition of a new discipline. Others have argued, notably at Stanford, that its natural home is within an interdisciplinary program of comparative studies in race and ethnicity.

That some students of Asian American origin apparently do not regard Asian studies programs as answering their needs was shown in a two-week protest in 1994, attended by strikes and seizing of administrative offices, at Columbia University. Prominent among the leaders were students of Asian origin at the undergraduate Columbia College demanding Asian American studies classes. When it was pointed out that the college had more courses on Asia available to the small student body than did any other undergraduate college in the country, the protestors replied that those courses did not count; they were about history and culture in Asian countries, not about Asians in the United States. That this was probably not idiosyncratic is suggested by a comment by Bruce Koppel in a wide-ranging survey of Asian studies. He says that, in the future, Asian studies will be less about Asia and more about Asians in the United States.[42] One hopes not, but the danger of ghettoizing is present in the search for roots and for ethnic identity, reinforcing a sense that

Asian Americans are not in the mainstream of American life, when the evidence points the other way. As a critic of the demand for Asian American studies rather acidly argues, this "whimpering preoccupation with the location of home" can create fertile grounds for racism.[43]

An issue for both Asian studies and Asian American studies that has arisen occasionally in the past, and that may become more insistent, is the demand, so prominent in the rise of black studies, that courses dealing with other cultures should be taught by faculty recruited on the basis of ethnic origin. This is, of course, the insider-outsider battle that has been so often and so inconclusively waged. In the case of black studies, the case for the insider seems at present to be widely accepted, but in Asian studies, if not in Asian American studies, there does not appear to be consensus in favor of the insider. Occasionally one hears the argument being made by someone not in any of the Asian fields that a candidate of Chinese descent will have a special insight into Indian culture by virtue of being "Asian," but Asians themselves would seldom make such a cross-cultural assumption. At the same time as we reject such simplicities, some Asian intellectuals, especially Indians, are scornful of much Western scholarship on Indian religion and culture. They reject what they regard as "the universalizing metanarratives" of Western scholars, with "a corresponding willingness to grant value to 'local knowledges' which take sustenance from the particular ways in which they are positioned in history and society."[44] This subject is never free from personal embarrassment and racial bias on both sides, and in the end the only answer, however unsatisfactory it may be, is that academic credentials and ability as a teacher, as in all fields, are self-validating. Up to the present, there has been a fairly general recognition in Asian studies that the pluralism of democratic societies is about the breaking down of barriers, not of erecting new ones. Asian studies, as traditionally practiced at liberal arts colleges, has been remarkably successful at doing just that, and while it is recognized that insiders may bring local knowledge, they may also bring special pleading and the blinkers of committed belief.

World history is the third category of programs that intersect with Asian studies programs and, it is sometimes argued, is an effective replacement for them in a situation where resources are scarce. To move in this direction, however, is to undervalue and misunderstand the function of both of them in the liberal arts curriculum. Wherever it may be located in a particular institution, world history boldly stakes its claim to a place within departments of history, the academic units traditionally most resistant to departures from national boundaries as the units of historical study. The teaching of world history is new in American classrooms, like Asian studies being essentially a post–World War II phenomenon, and in its earliest stages tended to be summaries of different regional and national histories. It took a new direction after the influential work of William McNeill, who defined world history as the mapping of the human community.[45] This meant the study of the transformations of human society that took place throughout the world, with continual interaction between regions and continents, which in turn meant giving the regions of Asia a large place in the human story. Perhaps the most coherent courses are built on examining great themes such as state formation, the building of empires, the spread of universal religions, family patterns, and trade.

Giving scholarly substance to the grand themes of historical development in Asia makes all the more essential the detailed knowledge of time and place that is the proper domain of Asian studies. Even as we urge the value in studying other cultures, we are aware that inherent in our enterprise is the danger of essentialism, that is, the ascribing of reality to qualities that are believed to be embodied in a culture and to determine all aspects of its nature. A familiar example is the very frequent explanation of many features of Indian society that are regarded as retrograde by the modern West, such as the alleged mistreatment of women, illiteracy, the oppression of the most disadvantaged sectors of the community, poverty, and overpopulation, as due to the belief systems of Hinduism. It is easy enough for someone with specialist knowledge of Indian religion and Indian history to controvert such explanations, but they are very appealing to the learned as well as the unlearned.

Toward Integration: In Practice

The attempt to summarize where we have come from in Asian studies at liberal arts colleges, and to hazard a guess as to where we are going, has turned out, not surprisingly, to be a single task. Different programs have started at different places and with different goals, as most of the chapters in this volume have shown in one way or another, and will move toward different developments. But whatever byways have been taken in the past that ended in dead ends, and no matter how ambiguous some of the signs toward the future may be, one line from the past that continues toward the future is clear. What the pioneers in introducing Asian studies into the liberal arts curriculum intended was not to establish a new discipline but to introduce knowledge of Asia into a curriculum that focused on Western Europe and its extraordinary extension into North America. The establishment of Asian studies programs was, as Rita Kipp notes in chapter five, very often basically a way to organize faculty with common interests in areas of Asia, to marshal resources from various parts of the institution, and to raise money from outside sources. The search for funds for their programs by faculty members themselves was something quite new, for faculty in the established fields are rarely expected to fund their own courses and programs. This fundraising, which absorbed a great deal of the time of many scholars in Asian studies, at the undergraduate as much as at the graduate level, astonished scholars from Europe and Asia, for whom such activity was quite unknown. Liberal arts colleges where such activity was common appear to have developed closer ties with the wider community of government, foundations, and businesses, than those where it was less prominent. This will almost certainly be one of the continuing effects of Asian studies at the colleges.

Integration of Asian studies in the liberal arts curriculum was stressed in the past, but more strenuous efforts will be needed to stabilize the achievements of programs and to maintain momentum for developing innovative programs to meet new challenges. Goals such as the globalization and internationalizing of education are becoming increasingly common, and while such efforts are to be applauded, the aims of some of the spokesmen for these efforts are not altogether identical with those of Asian studies programs. Thus a report of the American Council of Education (ACE) in 1996 notes that "unless today's students develop the competence to function effectively in a global environment, they are unlikely to succeed in the 21st century."[46] Programs in Asian studies have stressed the social sciences and the humanities, and the values that will come from their integration into the curriculum, but the ACE statement seems to scant the inherent value of such studies in favor of those that will make the nation prosper in the new century. Truth to tell, those of us who have engaged in fundraising for our cause have at times used such language, but surely our subtext was always a belief that Asian studies enriched the lives of students and faculty, and hence the larger society. The motivations for the introduction of Asian studies courses, as noted in this and other chapters in this volume, were many and varied, but they can perhaps be summarized, in Thomas Coburn's words in chapter one, as a yearning "for help in living amid the complexities of our increasingly *American-and-Asian* world." Another motivation, implicit in chapter two by Samuel Yamashita, is that Asian studies programs are part of the legacy of the spiritual vision of nineteenth-century America to take a message to the outside world. At the beginning of the twenty-first century the sense of mission is to have our students share in the heritage of Asian civilizations. One of the curious differences one can detect between teachers of Asian studies at liberal arts college and teachers of other subjects is this sense of mission. Its existence gives urgency and vitality to our promotion of Asian studies.

Continued integration of Asian studies, building on the past, will depend on at least six kinds of activity to be encouraged by Asian studies programs, five of which are developments within existing structures of the curriculum. All of them have been touched upon in various chapters of this book, and underlying all of them is the insistent recognition that the common culture of which we speak so often in defining liberal education must include the cultures of Asia as part of our intellectual heritage. This does not mean "decentering" the West, but finding a center that corresponds to the reality of the world.

One way of integrating Asian studies into the curriculum that was common at the beginning of our enterprise, but has perhaps gone out of favor, is the two-semester course. Encompassing at least three of the areas of Asia, usually China, Japan, and India, such a course parallels the familiar Western civilization offering. Two such sequences are possible. One can emphasize social and political development, in a chronological framework, with considerable attention to intellectual history. The other can be parallel courses in the humanities, on literature or art, which are often popular with both students and teachers. Those of us who have taught in such courses, thankfully usually with fellow specialists, can testify how difficult it is to make them coherent, but how rewarding they can be when they open new intellectual vistas to students and faculty. Few such courses include the rest of geographic Asia—Southeast Asia, Southwestern Asia, and Central Asia—but one could devise such a course with, for example, trade, the spread of the great religions, the transmission of culture, and the building of empires as linking themes. A number of points must be made about such courses. One is that the supply of scholars trained in various aspects of Asian societies is now such that those concerned with instituting them should be able to insist that they be taught by teachers with the same credentials as required for other kinds of courses. A second point, coverage, the specter that haunts so much of academia, should be exorcized by a concern for thematic depth, just as it should in a general course in Western civilization. A third point: such courses should not be thought of as surveys or introductions, but as self-sufficient offerings that can be part of any student's education. While they will provide depth and background for a disciplinary course, they must be related to the larger concerns of liberal education.

The second development that is now well under way and will become increasingly common is the introduction of courses centering on specific regions of Asia into existing disciplinary departments. When Asian studies were being introduced, there was great emphasis on interdisciplinary work as the wave of the future, but it is now clear, for better or for worse, that disciplines will remain the basis of the academic enterprise. This means that those of us involved in Asian studies must work from within disciplinary departments to claim a share of resources. Unthinkable though it may seem to some, when hard budget choices must be made a course in Chinese history—even one on South Asia—might win out over one in American history if rational choices are made. It is hard to imagine that in the future good departments, say, in art history or comparative literature, will not have a place for the incomparable legacies of the various Asian civilizations. As for religion, surely there is no department that does not recognize that all the dynamic religions of the modern world began in some corner of Asia and are imbued with the civilizations that nourished them. The struggle will be to make certain that courses dealing with Asia are not add-ons, but integral to disciplinary programs.

A third development that must be undertaken is the incorporation of Asian material into many existing courses, both in the social sciences and the humanities, that have traditionally concerned themselves only with material drawn from Western civilization. At a conference some years ago when this issue was being discussed, a scholar answered the question, "How can we include Asia in our courses?" by saying that the question was wrongly phrased. It should be, "How could one avoid including Asian material in core social science courses?"[47] Comparisons are natural in both the social sciences and the humanities. The difficulty is making the comparisons based on assured control of sources and without imposing criteria from the West on other cultures where they may not be relevant. Being aware of that danger, however, a teacher can find materials on Japan, for example, for comparisons in such areas as political participation, issues of race and class, labor-management relations, and the nature of bureaucracy.

One of the most fruitful ways to bring material from different Asian cultures into the classroom is through courses organized around issues and themes such as human rights, urbanism, imperialism, decolonization, gender, or state formation. Examination of such themes does not confine the teacher to the modern era, for all these themes resonate throughout history. How wide a net can be cast is indicated by a request on the Internet for help in preparing a course on gender roles in India that would include family, marriage, widowhood, birth control, abortion, employment, poverty, education, classical and contemporary art, advertisements, films, and TV. Twenty years ago, no one would have dreamed of such a course. In moving in this direction, teachers obviously will need help from disciplinary specialists in Asian studies, which in this case was quickly forthcoming, thanks to easy electronic communication. A step in helping nonspecialists integrate Asian material into disciplinary frameworks has been taken with the publication of a series of essays in the social sciences, literature, and history, by almost 100 scholars, in a project known as "Asia in the Core Curriculum." The books are specifically intended, not as texts for courses on Asian studies as such, but for integrating material into the disciplinary courses in the curriculum.[48]

Of all thematic issues, human rights presents the greatest challenge, and the greatest rewards, for introducing Asian material in the curriculum. This is because an exploration of human rights based on the United Nations covenants requires serious consideration of the meaning of rights in different cultural traditions, which means asking questions about historical and social developments. The questions are as simple as the answers are complex: Are there universal human rights, common to all people everywhere? Or are rights to be understood in terms of cultural relativism? Nadine Gordimer, the South African novelist, has described the UN Universal Declaration of Human Rights as "the touchstone, the creed of humanity, that surely sums up all other creeds directing human behaviour."[49] There is, however, very important dissent from a wide variety of Asian spokesmen. The Chinese, the Indian, and the Indonesian governments, for example, in various international gatherings have argued that their cultures have their own concepts of rights, and that the definitions in the UN covenants, with their claims to universality, cannot be sustained since they are derived from the

West. Nor should one forget the strong opposition to the Declaration of Human Rights in American circles. Michael Ignatieff has pointed out that American secretaries of state, from John Foster Dulles to Henry Kissinger, have regarded the human rights documents "as a tedious obstacle to the pursuit of great power politics."[50]

Western scholars tend to find the origin of modern human rights in the eighteenth century Enlightenment, with its emphasis on the individual, while spokesmen for the various Asian traditions argue for the priority of the community, at the most ancient level of their traditions, in defining their interpretations of the international covenants. Does this imply that there is no possibility for a dialog across cultures? Many of us who are involved in Asian studies and human rights will insist that an affirmative answer, based on deep knowledge of other cultures, is possible, and that this is at the heart of a whole enterprise in which the liberal arts college is engaged. There are no easy answers, but one that those involved in Asian studies should be able to give with clarity is that these Asian governments do not speak for all their people on moral issues, any more than the U.S. government speaks for all its citizens. Those who argue from a position of cultural relativism, for example, say that female circumcision should not be condemned, because it is approved by some African cultures, or that apartheid should not be condemned because it was legal practice under South African law. Such arguments ignore the fact that the most vigorous opposition to such practices very often come from within the societies themselves. In India, the defenders of women's rights are, for example, without exception, Indian men and women. In China, many individuals have suffered greatly for claiming the universality of fundamental human rights, in defiance of their government. They argue neither from the premises of East or West but from what it means to be human anywhere. Courses in Asian studies may discover that sexual practices and the control of the libido differ greatly between societies and indeed within societies but this does not mean that such issues do not belong to the essence of morality.[51] They may also discover that, even if it could be shown that the treatment of women by the Taliban in Afghanistan was enjoined by Islamic law, this would not prevent groups within or outside the society from denouncing it as against the rights of women as human beings. One of the benefits of a comparative study of human rights is that it may bring a freedom from believing that religious beliefs and practices should not be criticized. The great strength of Asian studies in the field of human rights may be to suggest that purely secular ethics can insist that no appeal to religion can justify inhuman treatment to any human being.

A fifth development, the study of Asian languages, is necessary for the true integration of Asian studies into the liberal arts college. This is not to suggest that every student who takes an Asian course should be required to take an Asian language—that would be as absurd and self-defeating as to require an undergraduate who takes a course in European history to know the languages of the area being studied. Asian studies programs, as Stanley Mickel argues in chapter three, should, however, attempt through formal language training on campus, as well as study abroad, to show that language is at the core of a culture, forcing a student to come to terms with the differences and similarities between cultures. Facilities for study in Asian countries are more difficult to arrange than the more familiar study abroad programs in Europe, but they can be immensely rewarding if combined with language and appropriate courses. Stephen Nussbaum includes in chapter four the cautionary reminder that, so far, programs in Asian countries have not found stable institutional homes, the basic requirement for successful programs.

The sixth activity that Asian studies programs should encourage is not particularly new and is known by the somewhat peculiar name of "outreach," which fits the sense of mission that characterizes many liberal arts colleges. One has the impression that Asian studies programs at colleges have not perhaps been as active as they might have been in reaching out to their communities to interest them in Asia and to inform them of the relevance of the history and cultures of the different nations in relation to American foreign policy. American colleges and universities have enormous resources of information, unmatched in any other country in the world, but these are not being shared with the business community, the media, and government at all levels. American churches, so important in the formation of attitudes toward other cultures, are also woefully uninformed and misinformed. The need in all these areas was dramatized, unhappily, in a news story in the summer of 1999, a time when it was desperately important that as a nation we understand movements and attitudes in the Islamic world. A functionary of the Senate Republican Policy Committee, with the serious-sounding designation of "foreign policy staff analyst," informed an audience that Islam has a "fraudulent self-depiction as a pacific creed," whereas it arises from "the darkness of heathen Araby," and is a "gigantic Christian-killing machine."[52] It is disquieting that only Muslims and specialists in Islamic studies appear to have denounced this bigotry in high places, suggestive proof of the darkness of late-twentieth-century America that scholars of Asian studies need to dispel. Where this has to be done is not among the students of Islam and the Middle East in our graduate schools but among the undergraduates who will be the best-informed elements in the constituencies of politicians and who will insist that public office requires respect for truth.

All these activities and developments in Asian studies enrich and deepen the historic mission of the American liberal arts college. They will continue to help in providing an intellectual and social milieu in which students and faculty can learn what their capabilities are, how these can be fulfilled, and how they may become responsible and productive citizens of a democratic society. The inadequacies of colleges in bringing this mission to fruition are many, and would not be denied by anyone with a close knowledge of American higher education. At the same time, there will be the recognition, as stated at the beginning, that this country has been well served by its liberal arts colleges, perhaps better than in any other nation. No small part of that service has been in making what Ezra Stiles called "the wisdom and literature of the East" part of our inheritance that may "illumine the world with justice and liberty."

Notes

1. Hsün Tzu, "Chapter 22: On the Correct Use of Terminology," 125.
2. Steven Koblick, "Foreword," XIV.
3. Harvard University, *General Education in a Free Society*, 4.
4. S.N. Mukerjee, *Sir William Jones*, 81.
5. Edward W. Said, *Orientalism*.
6. For example, Homi K. Bhabha, *Space, Postcolonial Times and the Trials of Cultural Translation*; and Gauri Viswanathan, *Masks of Conquest*.
7. Said, *Orientalism*, 3, 8.
8. James Clifford, *The Predicament of Culture*, 275.
9. Terry Lautz, personal communication, September 17, 1999.
10. Ainslie T. Embree, "The Tradition of Mission—Asian Studies in the United States, 1783 and 1983," 11–12.
11. Ezra Stiles, "The United States Elevated to Honor and Glory," 397–400.
12. See William Theodore de Bary and Tu Wei-ming, eds., *Confucianism and Human Rights*.
13. Charles O. Hucker, *The Association for Asian Studies*, 9.
14. "2000 Slate Announced," *Asian Studies Newsletter* 44.3 (Summer 1999), 5.
15. Milton Singer, ed., *Introducing India in Liberal Education*; H.G. Creel, ed., *Chinese Civilization in Liberal Education*.
16. Singer, *Introducing India in Liberal Education*, iv.

17. Horace Kallen, quoted in "Editor's Prologue," in Robert Orrill, ed., *Education and Democracy*, xvii.

18. John Dewey, quoted in ibid., xvii–xviii.

19. William Theodore de Bary, ed., A*pproaches to Oriental Classics*.

20. William Theodore de Bary and Irene Bloom, eds., *Approaches to the Asian Classics*, x.

21. William Theodore de Bary and Ainslie T. Embree, eds., *Approaches to Asian Civilizations*, vii.

22. Allan Bloom, *The Closing of the American Mind*, 33.

23. Robert A. McCaughey, *International Studies and Academic Enterprise*, 111–235.

24. Quoted in ibid., 127.

25. Christopher Shea, "Political Scientists Clash over Value of Area Studies," A13.

26. Ibid., A14.

27. Alan Ryan, *Liberal Anxieties and Liberal Education*, 149.

28. Richard H. Hersh, "The American College as the Place for Liberal Learning," 157.

29. Howard Gardner, *The Disciplined Mind*, 100–101.

30. Nathan Glazer, *We Are All Multiculturalists Now*, 1.

31. John Summerson, quoted in Herbert Muschamp, "A Bridge Between a City and Its Self-Image."

32. Amy Gutmann, "Introduction," in Charles Taylor et al., *Multiculturalism*, 9.

33. Henry Louis Gates, Jr., *Loose Canons*, 177.

34. Homi K. Bhabha, "Of Mimicry and Man: The Ambivalence of Colonial Discourse," in Bhabha, *The Location of Culture*, 85–92.

35. Charles Taylor, "The Politics of Recognition," 25.

36. John Morley, *Indian Speeches (1907–1909)*, 33.

37. Jürgen Habermas, "Struggles for Recognition in the Democratic Constitutional State," 107.

38. Quoted in Ainslie T. Embree, *Utopias in Conflict*, 60.

39. Troy Duster, "The Stratification of Cultures as the Barrier to Democratic Pluralism," 264–65.

40. Glazer, *We Are All Multiculturalists Now*, 1.

41. K. Anthony Appiah, "Identity, Authenticity, Survival," 149.

42. Bruce Koppel, *Refugees or Settlers?* 70.

43. Arif Dirlik, quoted in Somini Dasgupta, "Asian-American Programs Are Flourishing at Colleges."

44. John Stratton Hawley, "Who Speaks for Hinduism—and Who Against."

45. William H. McNeill, *The Rise of the West*.

46. *Educating Americans for a World in Flux*.

47. "A Place for Asia in the Undergraduate Core Curriculum in the 1980s."

48. Three volumes have been published by M.E. Sharpe (Armonk, NY): *Case Studies in the Social Sciences*, edited by Myron L. Cohen (1992); *Masterworks of Asian Literature in a Comparative Perspective*, edited by Barbara Stoler Miller (1994); and *Asia in Western and World History*, edited by Ainslie T. Embree and Carol Gluck (1997).

49. Quoted in Michael Ignatieff, "Human Rights," 58.

50. Ibid., 59.

51. Stuart Hampshire, "The Reason Why Not," 23.

52. *The Washington Post*, June 11, 1999, 14.

Bibliography

"A Place for Asia in the Undergraduate Core Curriculum in the 1980s." Report of a conference at Columbia University, New York, April 13–14, 1984.

Abu-Lughod, Lila. "Writing Against Culture." In Richard G. Fox, ed., *Recapturing Anthropology: Working in the Present*, 137–62. Santa Fe, NM: School of American Research Press, 1991.

ACTFL Proficiency Guidelines. Hastings-on-the-Hudson, NY: American Council on the Teaching of Foreign Languages, 1986.

Anderson, Benedict R. O'G. *Imagined Communities: Reflections on the Origin and Spread of Nationalism*. London: Verso, 1991.

Appiah, K. Anthony. "Identity, Authenticity, Survival: Multicultural Societies and Social Reproduction." In Charles Taylor et al., *Multiculturalism*, 149–63.

Astin, Alexander W. "How the Liberal Arts College Affects Students." In *Distinctively American*, 77–100.

Baccalaureate Origins of Doctoral Recipients: A Ranking by Discipline of 4-Year Private Institutions for the Period 1920–1995, 8th ed. Lancaster, PA: Franklin and Marshall College, in cooperation with the Higher Education Data Sharing Consortium, 1998.

Bennett, Wendell. *Area Studies in American Universities*. New York: Social Science Research Council, 1951.

Bhabha, Homi K. *The Location of Culture*. London: Routledge, 1994a.

———. *Space, Postcolonial Times and the Trials of Cultural Translation*. London: Routledge, 1994b.

Blake, Elizabeth. "The Yin and Yang of Student Learning in College." *About Campus* (September–October 1996): 4–9.

Bloom, Allan. *The Closing of the American Mind: How Higher Education Has Failed Democracy and Impoverished the Souls of Today's Students*. New York: Simon and Schuster, 1987.

Bonwell, Charles C., and James A. Eison. *Active Learning: Creating Excitement in the Classroom*. Washington, DC: George Washington University Press, 1991.

Borofsky, Robert. *Making History: Pukapukan and Anthropological Constructions of Knowledge*. Cambridge, England: Cambridge University Press, 1987.

Bourdieu, Pierre. *The Logic of Practice*. Stanford, CA: Stanford University Press, 1990.

Bowie, Katherine. *Rituals of National Loyalty: An Anthropology of the State and the Village Scout Movement in Thailand*. New York: Columbia University Press, 1997.

Boyer, Ernest. *Scholarship Reconsidered: Priorities of the Professoriate.* Princeton, NJ: Carnegie Foundation for the Advancement of Teaching, 1990.

Brann, Eva T.H. "The American College as *the* Place for Liberal Learning." In *Distinctively American,* 151–71.

Broad, Richard, and Bettina J. Huber. "Foreign Language Enrollments in United States Institutions of Higher Education, Fall 1995." In *The Modern Language Association of America, Document #713.* New York: MLA, 1997. Reprinted from *ADFL Bulletin* 28.2 (Winter 1997): 1–7.

Brumann, Christoph. "Writing for Culture." *Current Anthropology* 40 (February 1999): S1–S27.

Bruner, Jerome. *The Culture of Education.* Cambridge, MA: Harvard University Press, 1996.

Bulosan, Carlos. *America Is in the Heart: A Personal History.* New York: Harcourt Brace, 1946.

Burn, Barbara B. *Integrating Study Abroad into the Undergraduate Liberal Arts Curriculum.* Westport, CT: Greenwood, 1991.

Carlson, Ellsworth C. *Oberlin in Asia: The First Hundred Years 1882–1982.* Oberlin, OH: Oberlin Shansi Memorial Association, 1982.

Carnochan, W.B. *The Battleground of the Curriculum: Liberal Education and American Experience.* Stanford, CA: Stanford University Press, 1993.

Chatterjee, Partha. *Nationalist Thought and the Colonial World: A Derivative Discourse.* Minneapolis: University of Minnesota Press, 1986.

Ciolek, T. Matthew. "Asian Studies and the WWW: A Quick Stocktaking at the Cusp of Two Millennia." Web site *http://www.ciolek.com/PAPERS/pnc-taipei-98.html,* revised 1999.

Clifford, James. *The Predicament of Culture: Twentieth-Century Ethnography, Literature, and Art.* Cambridge, MA: Harvard University Press, 1988.

Coburn, Thomas B. "Cultural Memory and Postmodernism: A Pedagogical Note on Asian Studies." *Education About Asia* 1.1 (February 1996): 10–12.

———. "Nattering Nabobs, Habits of Mind, Persons in Relation: The Future of Liberal Arts Education in a Specialized Society." *Liberal Education* 7.1 (Spring 1985): 1–11.

Cohen, Myron L., ed. *Case Studies in the Social Sciences: A Guide for Teaching.* Armonk, NY: M.E. Sharpe, 1992.

Crapol, Edward P., and Howard Schonberger. "The Shift to Global Expansionism, 1865–1900." In William Appleman Williams, ed., *From Colony to Empire: Essays in the History of American Foreign Relations.* New York: Wiley, 1972.

Creel, H.G., ed. *Chinese Civilization in Liberal Education.* Chicago: University of Chicago Press, 1958.

Dasgupta, Somini. "Asian-American Programs Are Flourishing at Colleges." *New York Times,* June 9, 1999, A24.

Davis, Todd M., ed. *Open Doors 1997/98: Report on International Educational Exchange, 1998.* New York: Institute of International Education, 1998.

de Bary, William Theodore, ed. *Approaches to Oriental Classics.* New York: Columbia University Press, 1959.

———, ed. *Sources of Chinese Tradition,* one-vol. ed. New York: Columbia University Press, 1960a.

————, ed. *Sources of Chinese Tradition.* 2 vols. New York: Columbia University press, 1960b.

————, ed. *Sources of Indian Tradition*, 2d ed. 2 vols. New York: Columbia University Press, 1958, 1988.

————, ed. *Sources of Japanese Tradition.* 2 vols. New York: Columbia University press, 1958.

————, and Irene Bloom, eds. *Approaches to the Asian Classics.* New York: Columbia University Press, 1990.

————, and Ainslie T. Embree, eds. *Approaches to Asian Civilizations.* New York: Columbia University Press, 1964.

————, and Tu Wei-ming, eds. *Confucianism and Human Rights.* New York: Columbia University Press, 1997.

Distinctively American: The Residential Liberal Arts College. Special issue of *Daedalus* 128.1 (Winter 1999).

Duara, Prasenjit. *Rescuing History from the Nation: Questioning Narratives of Modern China.* Chicago: University of Chicago Press, 1995.

Duong Thu Huong. *Paradise of the Blind.* New York: Penguin, 1988.

Duster, Troy. "The Stratification of Cultures as the Barrier to Democratic Pluralism." In Robert Orrill, ed., *Education and Democracy*, 263–86.

Eck, Diana, and the Pluralism Project at Harvard University. *On Common Ground.* Interactive media. New York: Columbia University Press, 1997.

Edney, Matthew. *Mapping an Empire: The Geographical Construction of British India, 1765–1843.* Chicago: University of Chicago Press, 1997.

Educating Americans for a World in Flux: Ten Ground Rules for Internationalizing Higher Education. Washington, DC: American Council for Higher Education, 1996.

Embree, Ainslie T. "The Tradition of Mission—Asian Studies in the United States, 1783 and 1983." *Journal of Asian Studies* 43 (November 1983): 11–19.

————. *Utopias in Conflict: Religion and Nationalism in India.* New Delhi: Oxford University Press, 1992.

————, and Carol Gluck, eds. *Asia in Western and World History: A Guide for Teaching.* Armonk, NY: M.E. Sharpe, 1997.

Engerman, David C., and Parker G. Marden. *See* International Liberal Arts Colleges.

Engle, Lilli, and John Engle. "Study Abroad Levels: Notes Towards a Classification of Program Types." NAFSA (National Association for Foreign Student Affairs), Association of International Educators, conference paper, Denver, CO, May 1999.

Fairbank, John King. *Chinabound: A Fifty-Year Memoir.* New York: Harper & Row, 1982.

Feldman, Kenneth A. "Research Productivity and Scholarly Accomplishment of College Teachers as Related to Their Instructional Effectiveness: A Review and Exploration." *Research in Higher Education* 26 (1987): 227–98.

Fenton, William Nelson. *Area Studies in American Universities: For the Commission on Implications of Armed Services Educational Programs.* Washington, DC: American Council on Education, 1947.

Fernández-Armesto, Felipe. *Millennium: A History of the Last Thousand Years.* New York: Scribners, 1995.

Ford Foundation. *Crossing Borders: Revitalizing Area Studies.* New York: Ford Foundation, 1999.

Fosdick, Raymond. *The Story of the Rockefeller Foundation, 1913 to 1950.* New York: Harper & Row, 1952.

Frank, Andre Gunder. *ReOrient: Global Economy in the Asian Age.* Berkeley: University of California Press, 1998.

Freeman Foundation. *1998 Annual Report.*

Gaff, Jerry G., James L. Ratliff, and associates. *Handbook of the Undergraduate Curriculum: A Comprehensive Guide to Purposes, Structures, Practices, and Change.* San Francisco: Jossey-Bass, 1997.

Gardner, Howard. *The Disciplined Mind: What All Students Should Understand.* New York: Simon and Schuster, 1999.

Garon, Sheldon. *Molding Japanese Minds: The State in Everyday Life.* Princeton, NJ: Princeton University Press, 1997.

Gates, Henry Louis, Jr. *Loose Canons: Notes on the Culture Wars.* New York: Oxford University Press, 1992.

Geertz, Clifford. "From the Native's Point of View: On the Nature of Anthropological Understanding." In Jody Bennet Veroff and Nancy Rule Goldberger, ed., *The Culture and Psychology Reader.* New York: New York University Press, 1995, 25–40.

———. *The Interpretation of Cultures.* New York: Basic, 1973.

Geography Education Standards Project. *Geography for Life: National Geography Standards 1994.* Washington, DC: National Geographic Research and Exploration, 1994.

Glazer, Nathan. *We Are All Multiculturalists Now.* Cambridge, MA: Harvard University Press, 1997.

Gomes, Peter J. "Affirmation and Adaptation: Values and the Elite Residential College." In *Distinctively American*, 101–19.

Gonzalez, David. "John K. Fairbank, China Scholar of Wide Influence, Is Dead at 84." *New York Times*, September 16, 1991, B12.

Goody, Jack. *The East in the West.* Cambridge, England: Cambridge University Press, 1996.

Gordon, Leonard. *Doctoral Dissertations on China.* Seattle: University of Washington Press, 1972.

Gouda, Frances. *Dutch Culture Overseas: Colonial Practice in the Netherlands Indies, 1900–1942.* Amsterdam: Amsterdam University Press, 1995.

Griffiths, Stephen. *Emigrants, Entrepreneurs, and Evil Spirits: Life in a Philippine Village.* Honolulu: University of Hawaii Press, 1988.

Grinnell College Sesquicentennial Chinese Studies Committee. *Grinnell and China in the Twentieth Century.* Grinnell, IA: Grinnell College, 1996.

Grosse, Christine U., Walter V. Tuman, and Mary A. Critz. "The Economic Utility of Foreign Language Study." *Modern Language Journal* 82 (1998): 457–72.

Gutman, Amy. "Introduction." In Charles Taylor et al., *Multiculturalism*, 3–24.

Guzzardi, Walter. *The Henry Luce Foundation: A History, 1936–1986.* Chapel Hill: University of North Carolina Press, 1988.

Habermas, Jürgen. "Struggles for Recognition in the Democratic Constitutional State." In Charles Taylor et al., *Multiculturalism*, 107–48.

Hadley, Alice Omaggio. *Teaching Language in Context*, 2d ed. Boston: Heinle & Heinle, 1993.

Hall, John W. "Beyond Area Studies." In Donald E. Thackery, ed., *Research—Defini-*

tion and Reflections: Essays on the Occasion of the University of Michigan's Sesquicentennial. Ann Arbor, MI: University of Michigan Press, 1967, 48–66.

———. "East, South and Southeast Asia." In Michael Kammen, ed., *The Past Before Us: Contemporary Historical Writing in the United States.* Ithaca, NY: Cornell University Press, 1980, 156–86.

Hamm, Thomas. *Earlham College: A History 1847–1997.* Bloomington: Indiana University Press, 1997.

Hampshire, Stuart. "The Reason Why Not." *New York Review of Books* 46.7 (April 22, 1999) 21–23.

Hartman, John. "Thai Language Learning Framework and Forum," Web site *http://www.seasite.niu.edu/Thai/ThaiLLF/Default.htm#IV.*

Hartwell, Robert. "The Study of Literary Chinese." *Journal of the History of Education* 35 (1964): 434–41.

Harvard University. *General Education in a Free Society: Report of the Harvard Committee.* Cambridge, MA: Harvard University Press, 1945.

Hawaii Nikkei History Editorial Board, comp. *Japanese Eyes American Heart: Personal Reflections of Hawaii's World War II Nisei Soldiers.* Honolulu: Tendai Educational Foundation, 1998.

Hawley, John Stratton (Barnard College). "Who Speaks for Hinduism—and Who Against." Unpublished paper, 1999.

Hefner, Robert W., ed. *Democratic Civility: The History and Cross-Cultural Possibility of a Modern Political Ideal.* New Brunswick: Transaction, 1998a.

———, ed. *Market Cultures: Society and Morality in the New Asian Capitalisms.* Boulder, CO: Westview, 1998b.

Herman, Theodore. "Colgate University." In Ward Morehouse, ed., *Asian Studies in Liberal Arts Colleges,* 19–24.

Hersh, Richard H. "Generating Ideals and Transforming Lives: A Contemporary Case for the Residential Liberal Arts College." In *Distinctively American,* 173–94.

Hershatter, Gail, Emily Honig, Jonathan N. Lipman, and Randall Stross, eds. *Remapping China.* Stanford, CA: Stanford University Press, 1996.

Hershey, Charlie Brown. *Colorado College 1874–1949.* Colorado Springs: Colorado College, 1952.

Hirschman, Charles. "The State of Southeast Asian Studies in American Universities." In Charles Hirschman, Charles F. Keyes, and Karl Hutterer, with G. Carter Bentley, *Southeast Asian Studies in the Balance: Reflections from America.* Ann Arbor, MI: Association for Asian Studies, 1982, 41–58.

Hockett, Charles. *The State of the Art.* The Hague and Paris: Mouton, 1968.

Hsun Tzu. "Chapter 22: On the Correct Use of Terminology." In William Theodore de Bary, ed., *Sources of Chinese Tradition* (one-vol. ed.), 125–27.

Hucker, Charles. *The Association for Asian Studies: An Interpretive History.* Seattle: University of Washington Press, 1973.

Huntington, Samuel P. *The Clash of Civilizations and the Remaking of World Order.* New York: Simon and Schuster, 1996.

Hy Van Luong. " 'Brother' and 'Uncle': An Analysis of Rules, Structural Contradictions, and Meaning in Vietnamese Kinship." *American Anthropologist* 86.2 (June 1984): 290–315.

Ignatieff, Michael. "Human Rights: The Midlife Crisis." *New York Review of Books* 46.9 (May 20, 1999), 58–59.

International Liberal Arts Colleges. *In the International Interest: The Contributions and Needs of America's International Liberal Arts Colleges.* Written by David C. Engerman and Parker G. Marden. Beloit, WI: International Liberal Arts Colleges, 1992.

Jamieson, Neil L. *Understanding Vietnam.* Berkeley: University of California Press, 1993.

Jarchow, Merrill E., and Leal A. Headly. *Carleton, the First Century.* Northfield, MN: Carleton College, 1966.

Jeyaretnam, Philip. *Abraham's Promise.* Honolulu: University of Hawaii Press, 1995.

Johnston, Joseph S., Jr., and Jane R. Spalding. "Internationalizing the Curriculum." In Jerry G. Gaff et al., *Handbook of the Undergraduate Curriculum*, 416–35.

José, F. Sionil. *Dusk, a Novel.* New York: Modern Library, 1998.

Kahn, Joel. "Culture: Demise or Resurrection?" *Critique of Anthropology* 9 (1989): 5–25.

Kane, Joseph Nathan. *Famous First Facts: A Record of First Happenings, Discoveries, and Inventions in American History*, 4th ed. New York: Wilson, 1981.

Kauffman, Norman L., Judith N. Martin, and Henry D. Weaver, with Judy Weaver. *Students Abroad, Strangers At Home: Education for a Global Society.* Yarmouth, ME: Intercultural, 1992.

Keesing, Roger. "Theories of Culture Revisited." In Robert Borofsky, ed., *Assessing Cultural Anthropology.* New York: McGraw Hill, 1994, 301–12.

Kodansha Encyclopedia of Japan, vol. 5. Tokyo and New York: Kodansha, 1983.

Koblick, Steven. "Foreword." In *Distinctively American*, XIII–XIV.

Koppel, Bruce. *Refugees or Settlers? Area Studies, Development Studies, and the Future of Asian Studies.* Honolulu: East-West Center Occasional Papers, 1995.

Kublin, Hyman. "Brooklyn College." In Ward Morehouse, ed., *Asian Studies in Liberal Arts Colleges*, 11–18.

Lambert, Richard D. *International Studies and the Undergraduate.* Washington, DC: American Council on Education, 1989.

———. *Language and Area Studies Review.* Philadelphia: American Academy of Political and Social Science, 1973.

Landes, David. *The Wealth and Poverty of Nations: Why Some Are So Rich and Others So Poor.* New York: W.W. Norton, 1998.

Lang, Eugene M. "Distinctively American: The Liberal Arts College." In *Distinctively American*, 133–50.

Lautz, Terrill. "Financing Contemporary China Studies." In David Shambaugh, ed., *American Studies of Contemporary China.* Washington, DC: Woodrow Wilson Center; Armonk, NY: M.E. Sharpe, 1993, 301–14.

Leach, Edmund. *Claude Levi-Strauss*, rev. ed. New York: Penguin, 1974.

Lewis, Martin W., and Kären E. Wigen. *The Myth of Continents: A Critique of Metageography.* Berkeley: University of California Press, 1997.

Lindbeck, John. *Understanding China: An Assessment of American Scholarly Resources.* New York: Praeger, 1971.

Lyon, E. Wilson. *The History of Pomona College 1887–1969.* Claremont, CA: Pomona College, 1977.

Lyotard, Jean-François. *The Postmodern Condition.* Minneapolis: University of Minnesota Press, 1984.

McCaughey, Robert. *International Studies and Academic Enterprise: A Chapter in the Enclosure of American Learning.* New York: Columbia University Press, 1984a.

———. "International Studies and General Education: The Alliance Yet to Be." *Liberal Education* 70 (1984b): 343–74.

McNeill, William H. *The Pursuit of Power: Technology, Armed Force, and Society Since A.D. 1000.* Chicago: University of Chicago Press, 1982.

———. *The Rise of the West: A History of the Human Community.* Chicago: University of Chicago Press, 1963.

McPherson, Michael S., and Morton Owen Schapiro. "The Future Economic Challenges for the Liberal Arts Colleges." In *Distinctively American,* 47–75.

Magat, Richard. *The Ford Foundation at Work: Philanthropic Choices, Methods and Style.* New York: Plenum, 1979.

Marr, David G. Review of *Understanding Vietnam,* by Neil L. Jamieson. *Journal of Asian Studies* 53 (1994): 1005–07.

Matthews, Roberta S., Barbara Leigh Smith, Jean MacGregor, and Faith Gabelnick. "Creating Learning Communities." In Jerry G. Gaff et al., *Handbook of the Undergraduate Curriculum,* 457–75.

Mestenhauser, Josef A., Gayla Marty, and Inge Steglitz, eds. *Culture, Learning, and the Disciplines: Theory and Practice in Cross-Cultural Orientation.* Washington, DC: NAFSA (National Association for Foreign Student Affairs), 1988.

Meyers, Chet, and Thomas B. Jones. *Promoting Active Learning: Strategies for the College Classroom.* San Francisco: Jossey-Bass, 1993.

Michalak, Stanley L., Jr., and Robert J. Friedrich. "Research Productivity and Teaching Effectiveness in a Small Liberal Arts College." *Journal of Higher Education* 52 (1981): 578–97.

Miller, Barbara Stoler, ed. *Masterworks of Asian Literature in Comparative Perspective.* Armonk, NY: M.E. Sharpe, 1994.

Miller, Jacquie, and Jonathan Gatehouse. "Rainbow Families." *Gazette* (Montreal) October 12, 1997, D3.

Miura, Akira. "Japanese Language Teaching in the U.S.A.: A Historical Overview." *Breeze Quarterly* no. 18 (Fall 1998): 1–9.

Morehouse, Ward, ed. *American Institutions and Organizations Interested in Asia: A Reference Dictionary.* New York: Tatlinger, 1961a.

———, ed. *Asian Studies in Liberal Arts Colleges.* Washington, DC: Association of American Colleges, 1961b.

Morley, John. *Indian Speeches (1907–1909).* London: Macmillan, 1909.

Mukerjee, S.N. *Sir William Jones: A Study in Eighteenth Century British Attitudes to India.* Cambridge, England: Cambridge University Press, 1968.

Muschamp, Herbert. "A Bridge Between a City and Its Self-Image." *New York Times,* June 13, 1999, sect. 2, 37.

Nollen, John Scholte. *Grinnell College.* Iowa City: State Historical Society of Iowa, 1953.

Notestein, Lucy Lilian. *Wooster of the Middle West.* 2 vols. Kent, OH: Kent State University Press, 1937, 1971.

Nussbaum, Martha. *Cultivating Humanity: A Classical Defense of Reform in Liberal Education.* Cambridge, MA: Harvard University Press, 1997.

O'Connor, Stanley. "Humane Literacy and Southeast Asian Art." *Journal of Southeast Asian Studies* 26 (1995): 147–58.

Orrill, Robert, ed. *Education and Democracy: Re-Imagining Liberal Learning in America*. New York: College Entrance Examinations Board, 1997.

Palat, Ravi Arvind. "Fragmented Visions: Excavating the Future of Area Studies in a Post-American World." *Review* 19 (1996): 269–315.

Perry, William B., Jr. *Forms of Intellectual and Ethical Development in the College Years*. New York: Holt, Rinehart, and Winston, 1968.

Peterson's Study Abroad 1998. Princeton, NJ: Peterson's, 1999.

Pomona College Bulletin, Annual Catalogue, 1940–41. Claremont, CA: Pomona College, 1940.

Pomona College Bulletin, Annual Catalogue, 1945–46. Claremont, CA: Pomona College, 1945.

Pramoedya Ananta Toer. *See* Toer, Pramoedya Ananta.

Price, Carl. *Wesleyan's First Century*. Middletown, CT: Wesleyan University Press, 1932.

Project Kaleidoscope (PKAL). Web site *http://www.pkal.org*.

Readings, Bill. *The University in Ruins*. Cambridge, MA: Harvard University Press, 1996.

Reid, Anthony. *Southeast Asia in the Age of Commerce, 1450–1680*, vol. 1: *The Land Below the Winds*. New Haven, CT: Yale University Press, 1988.

———. "Studying 'Asia' Internationally." *IIAS Newsletter* no. 17 (December 1998): 5, 53.

Reischauer, Edwin O. *My Life Between Japan and America*. New York: Harper & Row, 1986.

Ritchie, William C., and Tej K. Bhatia, eds. *Handbook of Second Language Acquisition*. San Diego, CA: Academic, 1996.

Rodseth, Lars. "Distributive Models of Culture: A Sapirian Alternative to Essentialism." *American Anthropologist* 100.1 (March 1998): 55–69.

Rudolph, Frederick. *The American College and University: A History*. New York: Knopf, 1962.

Ryan, Alan. *Liberal Anxieties and Liberal Education*. New York: Hill and Wang, 1998.

Sahlins, Marshall. *Islands of History*. Chicago: University of Chicago Press, 1985.

Said, Edward W. *Orientalism*. New York: Pantheon, 1978.

Schmidt, George P. *The Liberal Arts College: A Chapter in American Cultural History*. New Brunswick, NJ: Rutgers University Press, 1957.

Scott, James C. *The Moral Economy of the Peasant: Rebellion and Subsistence in Southeast Asia*. New Haven, CT: Yale University Press, 1976.

———. *Seeing Like a State: How Certain Schemes to Improve the Human Condition Have Failed*. New Haven, CT: Yale University Press, 1998.

———. *Weapons of the Weak: Everyday Forms of Peasant Resistance*. New Haven, CT: Yale University Press, 1985.

Seidensticker, Edward. *Kafū the Scribbler.* Palo Alto, CA: Stanford University Press, 1959.

Shea, Christopher. "Political Scientists Clash over Value of Area Studies." *Chronicle of Higher Education*, February 10, 1997, A13.

Shedd, Clarence. *Two Centuries of Student Christian Movements: Their Origins and Intercollegiate Life*. New York: Association Press, 1934.

Shulman, Frank J. *Doctoral Dissertations on Japan and Korea 1969–1979*. Seattle: University of Washington Press, 1982.

————. *Japan and Korea: An Annotated Bibliography of Doctoral Dissertations in Western Languages*. Chicago: American Library Association, 1970.

Singer, Milton, ed. *Introducing India in Liberal Education*. Chicago: University of Chicago Press, 1957.

Smith, Bardwell. "Asian Studies at Carleton." *North Central Association Quarterly* 43 (1969): 277–80.

Smith, Daryl G. et al. *Diversity Works: The Emerging Picture of How Students Benefit*. Washington, DC: The American Association of Colleges and Universities, 1997.

Smith, Jonathan Z. *Imagining Religion: From Babylon to Jonestown*. Chicago: University of Chicago Press, 1982.

Smith, William Cantwell. "The Role of Asian Studies in the American University." Plenary address, New York State Conference on Asian Studies, Colgate University, Hamilton, NY, 1975. Printed and distributed by the Fund for the Study of the Great Religions of the World, Colgate University.

Steen, Sara J., ed. *Academic Year Abroad 1998/99: The Most Complete Guide to Planning Academic Year Study Abroad*. New York: Institute of International Education, 1998.

————, ed. *Academic Year Abroad 1999/2000: The Most Complete Guide to Planning Academic Year Study Abroad*. New York: Institute of International Education, 1999.

Stiles, Ezra. "The United States Elevated to Honor and Glory," in J.W. Thornton, ed., *The Pulpit of the American Revolution*. Boston: Gould and Lincoln, 1860, 397–520.

Stocking, George W., Jr. *Race, Culture and Evolution: Essays in the History of Anthropology*. Chicago: University of Chicago Press, 1982.

Stolcke, Verena. "Talking Culture: New Boundaries, New Rhetorics of Exclusion in Europe." *Current Anthropology* 36.1 (February 1995): 1–24.

Stoler, Ann Laura. "Rethinking Colonial Categories: European Communities and the Boundaries of Rule." *Comparative Studies in Society and History* 31.1 (January 1989): 134–61.

Takaki, Ronald. *Strangers from a Different Shore: A History of Asian Americans*. New York: Penguin, 1989.

Taylor, Charles et al. *Multiculturalism: Examining the Politics of Recognition*, ed. Amy Gutman. Princeton, NJ: Princeton University Press, 1994.

Taylor, Charles. "The Politics of Recognition." In Charles Taylor et al., *Multiculturalism*, 25–73.

Taylor, K.W. "Surface Orientations in Vietnam: Beyond Histories of the Nation and Region." *Journal of Asian Studies* 57 (1998): 949–78.

Thomas, Nicholas. *Colonialism's Culture: Anthropology, Travel, and Government*. Princeton, NJ: Princeton University Press, 1994.

Thompson, John. "Among Indiana Colleges." In Ward Morehouse, ed., *Asian Studies in Liberal Arts Colleges*, 32–41.

Thongchai Winichakul. *Siam Mapped: A History of the Geo-Body of a Nation*. Honolulu: University of Hawaii Press, 1994.

Titus, David. "A Brief History of East Asian Studies at Wesleyan." In *The Mansfield Freeman Center for East Asian Studies*. Middletown, CT: Wesleyan University, n.d.

Toer, Pramoedya Ananta. *This Earth of Mankind*. New York: Morrow, 1990.

Tu Wei-ming. "Cultural China: The Periphery as the Center." *Daedalus* 120.2 (1991): 1–32.

Turner, Bryan S. *Orientalism, Postmodernism and Globalism*. New York: Routledge, 1994.

Veblen, Thorstein. *The Higher Learning in America*. New York: B.W. Huebsch, 1918.

Veysey, Laurence. "Stability and Experiment in the American Undergraduate Curriculum." In Carl Kayson, ed., *Content and Context: Essays on College Education*. New York: McGraw-Hill, 1973.

Viswanathan, Gauri. *Masks of Conquest: Literary Study and British Rule in India*. New York: Columbia University Press, 1989.

Visweswaran, Kamala. "Race and the Culture of Anthropology." *American Anthropologist* 100.1 (March 1998): 70–83.

Volunteers in Asia. *Trans-Cultural Study Guide*. Stanford, CA: Volunteers in Asia, 1975.

Waley, Arthur. *Three Ways of Thought in Ancient China*. Stanford, CA: Stanford University Press [1939].

Watson, James L., ed. *Golden Arches East: McDonald's in East Asia*. Stanford, CA: Stanford University Press, 1997.

Wolf, Eric R. *Europe and the People Without History*. Berkeley: University of California Press, 1982.

Wright, Arthur F. *Buddhism in Chinese History*. New York: Atheneum, 1967.

Yeats, W.B. *The Poems: A New Edition*, ed. Richard J. Finneran. New York: Macmillan, 1983.

Yu, Pauline. "The Course of the Particulars: Humanities in the University of the Twenty-First Century." In Thomas Bender, Stanley Chodorow, and Pauline Yu, *The Transformation of Humanistic Studies in the Twenty-First Century: Opportunities and Perils*. ACLS Occasional Papers no. 40. New York: American Council of Learned Societies, 1997, 21–29.

Index

Abosch, David, 34
A Critique of Metageography (Martin/ Wigen), 100
Affirmative action, 46, 47
African Americans, 139–41
Akita, George, 32–33
American Association of Colleges and Universities (AAC&U)
  curriculum strategies, 16–17
  diversity benefits, 8–9
  Japan Seminar, 18
American Council of Learned Societies, 29–30, 33, 35
American Council on the Teaching of Foreign Languages (ACTFL), 63–65
American Oriental Society (1842), 29, 128
Anderson, Benedict, 114
Andover Theological Seminary, 24
Andrew W. Mellon Foundation, 46, 72
Area studies, 12, 38–39, 132–33
ASIANetwork, ix–xii, 18, 124n.55
Asiatic Society (1784), 126
Association for Asian Studies (AAS), 129–30

Bailey, Jackson, 34, 44
Beech, Joseph, 26
Beloit College, 70
Berlitz, Joseph, 61
Brooklyn College, 35
Brower, Robert, 32
Buddhism, 11

Carleton College, 25, 26, 42–43, 46
Carlson, Ellsworth, 34
Carnegie Corporation, 39
Case Studies in the Social Sciences: A Guide for Teaching, 10
Center for Advanced Research on Language Acquisition (CARLA), 59, 60–61
Ch'en Shou-yi, 33
Chiang Ching-kuo Foundation, 45, 57, 72, 74n.5
China
  culture of, 103–4, 116
    Buddhism, 11
    multiculturalism, 136–37
  language study
    curriculum choice, 65–66
    historically, 56–57, 59, 61
    standards, 65
    student interest, 67
    study length, 66
    summer courses, 69, 70
Christianity. *See* Missionaries (1808–1930)
Clash of Civilization and the Remaking of World Order, The (Huntington), 109
Cold War
  Asian studies, 39–40
  language study, 57, 58
Cole, Allan, 33
Colorado College, 26, 27, 28

Columbia University
  Columbia Project on Asia in the Core
    Curriculum, 10
  Western Contemporary Civilization, 4,
    18
Community outreach, 148–49
Comparative learning, 7–8
Council on International Educational
  Exchange (CIEE), 60
*Çrossing Borders: Revitalizing Area
  Studies*, 12
Crowley, James, 34
Culture
  Asian studies development
    cultural change, 110–11
    cultural China, 103–4, 116
    cultural elements, 108–9
    cultural homogeneity, 107–8,
      116–17
    culture defined, 104–5
    as economic explanation, 109–10
    pedagogy implications, 116–17
    racism and, 105–7
  diversity of
    influence of, 9
    language study, 52–53
    liberal arts education, 8–9, 21n.13
  ethnic studies, 138–41
    African Americans, 139–41
    Asian Americans, 139–41
  mobility of, 12
  multiculturalism, 135–38
    China, 136–37
    India, 137–38
  racism and, 105–7
  religious
    Chinese Buddhism, 11
    contemporary American, 13
Curriculum inclusion
  Asian population, 12
  contemporary context, 12–15
    American religious culture, 13
    Asian population, 12
    cultural mobility, 12
    globalization, 12–13
    Western academy, 12–15

Curriculum inclusion
  contemporary context *(continued)*
    Western academy development,
      13–15
  culture and
    diversity of, 8–9, 21n.13
    mobility of, 12
    religious, 11, 13
  globalization, 12–13
  historical context, 3–4
    Asian studies (1946–60), 33, 34,
      35–36
    Asian studies expansion (1960–90),
      41–44, 47
    Asian studies rediscovery (1930–45),
      28, 30
    Chinese Buddhism, 11
    human heritage, 10–12
    Western academy, 10–12
    Western academy development,
      13–15
  language study, 65–67
    language choice, 65–66
    student interest, 66–67
  liberal arts colleges, 4–5, 15–20
    current courses, 23
    definition of, 5, 20n.6
    inclusion strategies, 16–20
    influence of, 5
    international perspective, 16
  liberal arts education, 6–10
    binary process of, 6–9
    comparative learning, 7–8
    cultural diversity, 8–9, 21n.13
    decentering perspective, 6, 20n.9
    ellipse perspective, 6–9
    pedagogy, 9–10
  overview, 3–5
  religious culture
    American, 13
    Chinese Buddhism, 11
  strategies for, 16–20, 142–49
    Asian-born faculty, 19
    autonomy vs. infusion, 17–18
    community outreach, 148–49
    course incorporation, 145–46

Curriculum inclusion
  strategies for *(continued)*
    disciplinary focus, 145
    global education, 143
    human rights study, 146–48
    language study, 148
    motivation, 143–44
    residential campuses, 19–20
    specialist vs. nonspecialist, 18–19
    two-semester course, 144–45
  Western academy, 10–15
    contemporary context, 12–15
    development of, 13–15
    historical context, 10–12
    objectivity obsession, 14
    theory preoccupation, 14–15

deBary, William, 32, 131
Decentering, Asian studies
  centered insularity, 114–15
  cultural impact, 116–17
  developmental directions, 111–18
  implications of, 112–14
  introductory course, 117–18
  liberal arts education, 6, 20n.9, 112–15,
    121–22
  pedagogy implications, 116–18
  reasons for, 111–12
  study abroad, 113–14
*Democratic Civility: The History and
  Cross-cultural Possibility of a
  Modern Political Ideal* (Hefner),
  110
Development, Asian studies
  Asian myth, 99–103
    East-West dichotomy, 99–100
    European ethnocentrism, 100–101,
      122n.8
    geography and, 100–101
    nation-state distinction, 102–3
  culture
    changing nature of, 110–11
    cultural China, 103–4, 116
    defined, 104–5
    as economic explanation, 109–10
    elements of, 108–9

Development, Asian studies
  culture *(continued)*
    homogeneity of, 107–8, 116–17
    pedagogy implications, 116–17
    racism and, 105–7
  decentering, 111–18
    centered insularity, 114–15
    cultural impact on, 116–17
    implications of, 112–14
    introductory course, 117–18
    liberal arts education, 6, 20n.9,
      112–15, 121–22
    pedagogy implications, 116–18
    reasons for, 111–12
    study abroad, 113–14
  ethnic studies, 138–41
    African Americans, 139–41
    Asian Americans, 139–41
  geography and, 99, 100–101, 118–20
  integration strategies, 142–49
    community outreach, 148–49
    course incorporation, 145–46
    disciplinary focus, 145
    global education, 143
    human rights study, 146–48
    language study, 148
    motivation for, 143–44
    two-semester course, 144–45
  intersection programs
    ethnic studies, 138–41
    multiculturalism, 135–38
    world history, 141–42
  multiculturalism, 135–38
    China, 136–37
    India, 137–38
  pedagogy implications, 120–22
    culture and, 116–17
    decentering Asian studies, 116–18
    humane literacy, 11, 113, 121
    introductory course, 117–18
    liberal arts college, 112–15, 121–22
  remapping
    geographically, 99
    institutionally, 98–99
    theoretically, 98
  world history programs, 141–42

Disciplined Mind: What All Students Should Understand, The (Gardner), 134
Distinctively American: Residential Liberal Arts College, 80
Diversity Works: The Emerging Picture of How Students Benefit, 9
Dodge Foundation, 57

East Asian Summer Languages Institute (EASLI), 69–70
Economics, Asian
 Asian studies expansion, 43
 cultural causality, 109–10
 language study, 56
 vs. European economics, 99–100
Edmunds, Charles, 27
Ethnic studies, 138–41
 African Americans, 139–41
 Asian Americans, 139–41
Europe
 economics of, 99–100
 ethnocentrism of, 100–101, 122n.8

Faculty
 administrative leadership, 43–45
 Asian studies support, 34–35
 curriculum inclusion, 19
 liberal arts education, 9–10
 retraining of, 35–36
 specialization
  area studies, 12, 38–39, 132–33
  Asian studies (1946–60), 33–34
  Asian studies expansion (1960–90), 40–41, 42–44, 47
  Asian studies fields (1960–70), 39–40
  Asian studies rediscovery (1930–45), 28–29, 31, 32–33
  vs. nonspecialists, 18–19
 study abroad
  collaboration value, 93–94
  language instructors, 87
  pedagogical methods, 90–92
  staff ratio, 92
 See also Pedagogy

Fahs, Charles, 30, 31
Fairbank, John, 30, 31
Far East Association (1941), 31, 37, 129
Far Eastern Quarterly, 37
Ford Foundation, 12, 18, 39, 45, 73, 132
Frank, Andre Gunder, 99–100
Freeman Foundation, 45, 73
Fund for the Improvement of Postsecondary Education (FIPSE), 73
Funding
 historical context
  Asian studies (1946–60), 34–35
  Asian studies expansion (1960–90), 45–46, 47
  Asian studies fields (1960–70), 37, 39–40
  Asian studies rediscovery (1930–45), 29–31, 33
 language study, 57, 74n.5
 National Defense Education Act (NDEA), 40, 45–46, 132
 See also specific foundations

Gardner, Howard, 134
General Association of Congregational Churches (Massachusetts), 24
General education requirements, 43, 47
Geography, 99, 100–101, 118–20
Globalization, 12–13, 16, 99–100, 143
Golden Arches East: McDonald's in East Asia (Watson), 109
Government
 Asian nation-state, 102–3
 language study programs, 40, 45–46, 57, 58, 74n.4, 132
 National Defense Education Act (NDEA), 40, 45–46, 132
 National Defense Foreign Language (NDFL), 40, 57, 58, 74n.4
Gowdy, John, 26
Graduate programs, 36–37, 132, 133–34
Grinnell College, 25

Harvard Journal of Asiatic Studies, 37
Hefner, Robert, 110

Henry Luce Foundation, xi, xiii, 39, 40, 45, 73
Hibbett, Howard, 32
Historical context
  area studies, 12, 38–39, 132–33
  Asian studies (1946–60), 33–36
    curriculum, 33, 34, 35–36
    faculty retraining, 35–36
    faculty support, 34–35
    funding, 34–35
    Indiana Project, 35–36
    specialization, 33–34
  Asian studies expansion (1960–90), 40–47
    administrative leadership, 43–45
    affirmative action, 46, 47
    Asian economics, 43
    curriculum, 41–44, 47
    funding, 45–46, 47
    general education, 43, 47
    immigration, 46, 47
    specialization, 40–41, 42–44, 47
  Asian studies fields (1960–70), 36–40
    area studies, 38–39
    Cold War influence, 39–40
    funding, 37, 39–40
    graduate programs, 36–37
    language study, 37
    publications, 37–38
    specialization, 39–40
  Asian studies rediscovery (1930–45), 28–33
    curriculum, 28, 30
    funding, 29–31, 33
    language study, 29, 30, 32–33
    specialization, 28–29, 31, 32–33
    World War II, 31–33
Chinese Buddhism, 11
chronologically
  1700s, 126–28
  1808–1930, 24–28
  1930–1945, 28–33
  1946–1960, 33–36
  1960–1970, 36–40
  1960–1990, 40–47
human heritage, 10–12

Historical context *(continued)*
  language study, 56–61
    Asian economics, 56
    Chinese, 56–57, 59, 61
    Cold War, 57, 58
    funding, 57, 74n.5
    government programs, 40, 45–46, 57, 58, 74n.4, 132
    Indian, 56, 59–60
    Japanese, 56, 58–59, 61
    Korean, 56, 59, 61
    1930–45, 29, 30, 32–33, 56, 57, 58
    1960–70, 37, 57, 58
    Pomona College, 56–57
    South Asian, 59–60, 61
    Southeast Asian, 60, 61
    World War II, 56, 58
    Yale University, 56
  missionaries (1808–1930), 24–28
    Asian students, 26–27
    campus societies, 24
    Christian educators, 24–25
    domestic movement, 25
    foreign missions, 24–26
    industry influence, 26
    missionary students, 27–28
    Progressivism, 26
    YMCA/YWCA chapters, 25
  organizations
    American Oriental Society (1842), 29, 128
    Asiatic Society (1784), 126–27
    ASIANetwork, ix–xii, 18, 124n.55
    Association for Asian Studies (AAS), 129–30
    Far East Association (1941), 31, 37, 129
    Institute of Pacific Relations (1925), 31, 129
    Oriental Education Commission (1909), 29
  overview, 3–4, 23–24, 47–48
  university conferences, 129–32
Western academy, 10–15
  development of, 13–15
  human heritage, 10–12

Human rights, 146–48
Huntington, Samuel, 109

Imagined Communities (Anderson), 114
Immersion programs, 70
  See also Study abroad
Immigration, 46, 47
Immigration Act (1965), 46
India
  language study
    historically, 56, 59–60
    student interest, 67
  multiculturalism, 137–38
Indiana Project, 35–36
Institute of Pacific Relations (1925), 31,
  129
Internet, language study, 59, 60–61, 65,
  68, 69–70, 72
Internships, language study, 70–71

Jamieson, Neil, 108–9
Japanese language
  curriculum choice, 65–66
  historically, 56, 58–59, 61
  standards, 65
  student interest, 67
  study length, 66
  summer courses, 69, 70
Japan Foundation, 45, 58, 73
Japan Seminar (AAC&U), 18
Jones, Edwin, 26
Jones, Sir William, 126–27
Journal of Asian Studies, 37
*Journal of the American Oriental
  Society*, 37

Kabayama, Ayskeh, 27
Kafū, Nagai, 27
Keene, Donald, 32
Korea Foundation, 73
Korean language
  curriculum choice, 66
  historically, 56, 59, 61
  student interest, 67
  study length, 66
  summer courses, 69

Krashen, Stephen, 62–63

Landes, David, 99
Language study
  Chinese
    curriculum choice, 65–66
    historically, 56–57, 59, 61
    standards, 65
    student interest, 67
    study length, 66
    summer courses, 69, 70
  curriculum development, 65–67, 148
    language choice, 65–66
    student interest, 66–67
  funding, 57, 72–74, 74n.5
  historical context, 56–61
    Asian economics, 56
    Chinese, 56–57, 59, 61
    Cold War, 57, 58
    funding, 57, 74n.5
    government programs, 40, 45–46,
      57, 58, 74n.4, 132
    Indian, 56, 59–60
    Japanese, 56, 58–59, 61
    Korean, 56, 59, 61
    1930–45, 29, 30, 32–33, 56, 57, 58
    1960–70, 37, 57, 58
    Pomona College, 56–57
    South Asian, 59–60, 61
    Southeast Asian, 60, 61
    World War II, 56, 58
    Yale University, 56
  Indian
    historically, 56, 59–60
    student interest, 67
  Japanese
    curriculum choice, 65–66
    historically, 56, 58–59, 61
    standards, 65
    student interest, 67
    study length, 66
    summer courses, 69, 70
  Korean
    curriculum choice, 66
    historically, 56, 59, 61
    student interest, 67

Language study
  Chinese *(continued)*
    study length, 66
    summer courses, 69
    pedagogical methods, 61–65
      audio-lingual, 62
      cognitive, 62–63
      communicative competence, 63
      direct, 61–62
      disadvantages of, 61–62
      grammar-translation, 61
      learning standards, 64–65
      monitor model, 62–63
      proficiency guidelines, 63–64
      silent, 63
    pedagogical structure, 67–71
      college courses, 68–69
      immersion programs, 70
      internships, 70–71
      self-study, 58, 61, 68
      study abroad, 70–71, 84–85, 87, 89, 90
      summer courses, 69–70
      videoconferences, 69
  South Asian
    curriculum choice, 66
    historically, 59–60, 61
    study length, 66
  Southeast Asian
    curriculum choice, 66
    historically, 60, 61
    study length, 66
  study abroad, 70–71, 84–85
    institutional plan for, 89, 90
    instructors, 87
    student fears, 95
  technology role, 69, 71–72
    videoconferences, 69
    Web sites, 59, 60–61, 65, 68, 69–70, 72
  value of, 52–56
    character writing system, 54
    cultural diversity, 52–53
    employment, 54–55
    intellectual development, 53–54
  Web sites, 59, 60–61, 65, 68, 69–70, 72

Latourette, Kenneth Scott, 28
Lee, Edwin, 34
Levenson, Joseph, 32
Lewis, Martin, 100–101
Liberal arts education
  Asian studies decentering, 6, 20n.9, 112–15, 121–22
  binary process of, 6–9
    comparative learning, 7–8
    cultural diversity, 8–9, 21n.13
    ellipse perspective, 6–9
  commonality of, 125
  cultural diversity, 8–9, 21n.13
    influence of, 9
  ellipse perspective, 6–9
  purpose of, 126
  study abroad, 79–83, 113–14
    demographics of, 80–81
    social context, 82–83
    value of, 80, 81
  See also Pedagogy
Lilly Foundation, 13, 44
Louis & Maud Hill Family Foundation, 46

Mary Reynolds Babcock Foundation, 46
Middlebury College, 69
Missionaries (1808–1930), 24–28
  Asian students, 26–27
  campus societies, 24
  Christian educators, 24–25
  domestic movement, 25
  foreign missions, 24–26
  industry influence, 26
  missionary students, 27–28
  Progressivism, 26
  YMCA/YWCA chapters, 25
Moore, Ray, 34
Moral Economy of the Peasant, The (Scott), 114
Multiculturalism, 135–38
  China, 136–37
  India, 137–38
Musser Endowment Fund, 46

Nagai, Kafū, 27
National Association of
    Self-Instructional Language
    Programs (NASILP), 58, 61, 68
National Defense Education Act
    (NDEA), 40, 45–46, 132
National Defense Foreign Language
    (NDFL), 40, 57, 58, 74n.4
National Endowment for the Humanities,
    46
Niijima, Jo, 26

Oberlin College, 25, 26–27, 28, 34
On Common Ground: World Religions in
    America, 13
Oriental Education Commission (1909), 29
Orientalism (Said), 19, 99, 127

Pedagogy
    Asian studies development, 120–22
        culture and, 116–17
        decentering, 116–18
        humane literacy, 11, 113, 121
        introductory course, 117–18
        liberal arts college, 112–15, 121–22
    language study
        audio-lingual, 62
        cognitive method, 62–63
        college courses, 68–69
        communicative competence, 63
        direct method, 61–62
        disadvantages of, 61–62
        grammar-translation, 61
        immersion programs, 70
        internships, 70–71
        learning standards, 64–65
        methods, 61–65
        monitor model, 62–63
        proficiency guidelines, 63–64
        self-study, 58, 61, 68
        silent method, 63
        structure, 67–71
        study abroad, 70–71, 84–85, 87, 89,
            90
        summer courses, 69–70
        videoconferences, 69

Pedagogy (continued)
    liberal arts education, 9–10
    specialization
        area studies, 12, 38–39, 132–33
        Asian studies (1946–60), 33–34
        Asian studies expansion
            (1960–90), 40–41, 42–44,
            47
        Asian studies fields (1960–70),
            39–40
        Asian studies rediscovery (1930–45),
            28–29, 31, 32–33
        vs. nonspecialists, 18–19
    study abroad, 90–92
        language study, 70–71, 84–85, 87,
            89, 90
    See also Faculty
Pew Charitable Trusts, 73
Pomona College, 30, 31, 33
    language study, 56–57
Population, 12
Project Kaleidescope, 10, 21n.18
Publications, 37–38
    See also specific publications

Racism, 105–7
Reischauer, Edwin, 30, 31, 32
Religious culture
    Chinese Buddhism, 11
    contemporary American, 13
    See also Missionaries (1808–1930)
ReOrient: Global Economy in the Asian
    Age (Frank), 99–100
Rockefeller Foundation, 29–31, 33, 35,
    39

Said, Edward, 19, 99, 127
School of International Training (SIT),
    60
Schwartz, Benjamin, 32
Scott, James, 114
Seidensticker, Edward, 32
Self-study, language, 58, 61, 68
Siam Mapped: A History of the
    Geo-Body of a Nation
    (Thongchai), 102

Smith, Wilfred Cantwell, 13–14
Society of Brethren, 24, 25
South Asian languages
  curriculum choice, 66
  historically, 59–60, 61
  study length, 66
Southeast Asian languages
  curriculum choice, 66
  historically, 60, 61
  study length, 66
Specialization
  area studies, 12, 38–39, 132–33
  Asian studies (1946–60), 33–34
  Asian studies expansion (1960–90),
    40–41, 42–44, 47
  Asian studies fields (1960–70), 39–40
  Asian studies rediscovery (1930–45),
    28–29, 31, 32–33
  vs. nonspecialists, 18–19
  See also Faculty; Pedagogy
Standards for Foreign Language
    Learning, 64–65
Starr Foundation, 73
Stiles, Ezra, 127–28
Study abroad
  Asian destinations, 78, 79
  challenges to, 89–96
    collaboration, 93–94
    institutional plan, 89–90
    on-site education, 90–92
    student issues, 94–96
  faculty
    collaboration, 93–94
    language instructors, 87
    pedagogical methods, 90–92
    staff ratio, 92
  historical development, 78
  host mothers, 87–88
  institutional comparison, 78–79
  institutional plan, 89–90
    language study, 89, 90
    long-term engagement, 89–90
    student recruitment, 90
  language study, 70–71, 84–85
    institutional plan, 89, 90
    instructors, 87

Study abroad
  language study *(continued)*
    student fears, 95
  liberal arts education, 79–83, 113–14
    demographics of, 80–81
    social context, 82–83
    value of, 80, 81
  liberal inquiry, 85–89
    compelling nature, 85–86
    cultural apprenticeship, 86–87
    long-term engagement, 87–88, 89–90,
      92
  social density, 83–85
    language study, 84–85
  students
    exploration bias, 94–95
    issues of, 94–96
    language skills, 95
    monitoring of, 95–96
    predeparture orientation, 95
    recruitment of, 90
    requirements of, 91–92
  value of, 76–77, 96
Summer courses, language, 69–70
  Chinese, 69, 70
  institutes for, 60, 69–70
  Japanese, 69, 70
  Korean, 69

Taft, Marcus Lorenzo, 24
Technology, language study, 69, 71–72
  videoconferences, 69
  Web sites, 59, 60–61, 65, 68, 69–70,
    72
Thongchai Winichakul, 102
*Transactions of the Asiatic Society of
    Japan*, 37
Tsuneishi, Warren, 32

Undergraduate International Studies
    in Foreign Language Program,
    73
Understanding Vietnam (Jamieson),
    108–9

Videoconferences, language study, 69

War influence
  Cold War
    Asian studies, 39–40
    language study, 57, 58
  World War II
    Asian studies, 31–33, 58
    language study, 56, 58
Watanabe, Tsune, 26
Watson, James L., 109
Wealth and Poverty of Nations: Why Some Are So Rich and Others So Poor, The (Landes), 99
Weapons of the Weak (Scott), 114
Web sites, language study, 59, 60–61, 65, 68, 69–70, 72
Wentworth, Erasmus, 24
Wesleyan University, 24, 26, 27
Western academy, 10–15
  contemporary context, 12–15

Western academy *(continued)*
  development of, 13–15
  historical context, 10–12
  objectivity obsession, 14
  theory preoccupation, 14–15
White, Francis Harding, 28
White, Moses, 24
Wigen, Kären, 100–101
William & Flora Hewlett Foundation, 74
Williams College, 24
World War II
  Asian studies, 31–33, 58
  language study, 56, 58

Yale University, 24
  language study, 56
Young Men's Christian Association (YMCA), 25
Young Women's Christian Association (YWCA), 25